D1434174

Enemies of Poetry

By the same author (with **R. B. McDowell**)

Mahaffy: a Biography of an Anglo-Irishman

Enemies of Poetry

W. B. Stanford

Routledge & Kegan Paul

London, Boston and Henley

First published in 1980
by Routledge & Kegan Paul Ltd
39 Store Street, London WC1E 7DD,
Broadway House, Newtown Road,
Henley-on-Thames, Oxon RG9 1EN and
9 Park Street, Boston, Mass. 02108, USA
Set in Monotype Baskerville
and printed in Great Britain by
Ebenezer Baylis & Son Ltd,
The Trinity Press, Worcester, and London
© W. B. Stanford 1980
ISBN 0 7100 0460 5

Contents

Our classical tradition has been strongest in the past when it was based four-square on poetry, oratory, history and philosophy. But when the balance between them is upset, then the whole system suffers. My own belief – but it is obviously biased – is that if the imaginative element, that is, the poetic element, in literature is disparaged and neglected – as it has sometimes been in the past – many young students will lose interest and turn to better cultivated literary fields. For example I know of no introduction to a great poem more likely to repel or misdirect a reader seeking to understand the *Iliad* as a poem about human emotions than Leaf's preface to his still standard edition, as I shall try to show later.

Almost all the axioms on which I base my replies to hostile criticism are derived from Aristotle's *Poetics*. I know that in some quarters it is fashionable to decry this work as a source of misunderstanding about classical poetry. One professor to my knowledge warns his literary students to avoid it entirely. All I can now say is that the more I study it the more I admire its masterly commonsense and penetrating insight. Though Aristotle was essentially a scientist and logician himself – his poem to *areté* would hardly have been preserved if an Aristotle had not written it – yet with an unbiased scientist's power of observation he saw the nature and purpose of poetry more clearly than any other literary critic in antiquity.

I have chosen the rather aggressive title *Enemies of Poetry* rather than something milder like *Misrepresentations and Fallacies in Classical Criticism* or *Animadversions on Certain Questionable Attitudes to Classical Poetry*, because 'enemies of poetry' is exactly what several eminent scholars of the last century have, in my opinion, essentially been, despite their protestations of reverence for the poets whom they have traduced or dismembered. Open enemies like Plato have often been answered, but enemies like Richard Bentley, Walter Leaf and, surprisingly, Gilbert Murray (in an early book) have not, I think, been clearly enough identified in the past.

I must make a careful distinction here between hostile and neutral attitudes to poetry among those classical critics who

Chapter One

Enemies of Poetry

In a time like the present when creative literature is being used more and more as material for history or archaeology or sociology or psychology it may be well for those who value creative literature for its own sake to defend fiction in general and poetry in particular in terms of their own aims and methods. There are two ways of doing this. One is positive – to repeat the principles of favourable literary criticism from Aristotle to Eliot. The other is negative – to identify and if possible to refute the main reasons why non-literary scholars and critics have so often misunderstood and misrepresented fictional writing, especially poetry. In what follows here I have mainly followed the *via negativa*, though necessarily I have referred to the basic canons of sympathetic criticism from time to time.

I have written on the whole as an advocate rather than as a judge. Critics such as Plato and Bentley and Leaf have said such outrageous things about poetry that I still find it hard to discuss their strictures dispassionately. If I have overstated the case at times, I apologize. But the antipoetic forces are still so strongly entrenched in classical studies that to make any lasting impression on them one must thrust hard. I hasten to add that I have no personal antipathy to the honourable disciplines – history, science, philosophy, psychology and politics – discussed in the following pages, so long as their advocates do not try to convert and assimilate poetry to their own purposes. All I assert – following Aristotle – is the uniqueness and autonomy of poetry.

Acknowledgments

My thanks are due to colleagues and friends who helped with information and advice – and warnings not always heeded – in this rather temerarious book: in mainly literary matters to A. E. Hinds, J. V. Luce, J. K. Walton and D. E. W. Wormell; in history to P. A. Cartledge; in science to D. A. Webb; in mathematics to D. A. Spearman; and in philosophy to J. V. Luce again. Others are mentioned in the notes. I am also grateful to Paulene Byrne for coping with the obscurities of my handwriting so patiently. I am particularly indebted to my wife who gave invaluable and untiring help in all stages of the work. Among the books in my short-title list I gained most from those by M. H. Abrams, Rosamond Harding, Rosemary Harriott, John Press and – just in time – Oliver Taplin.

are not themselves admirers of poetry. Obviously historians, scientists, philosophers, psychologists and politicians are entitled to study and use for their own purposes whatever a poet has published, since every poem is in a sense a historical document and a legitimate subject for scientific research. If critics of this kind recognize that poetry is an autonomous world of its own with its own laws and customs – as different at times from the world of science as China is from Peru – they can genuinely enrich our understanding of poetry and the poetic art. These unaggressive users of poetry are not the concern of the present book. They do not traduce or mutilate poetry when they are handling it. Naturally they often regard poetry as being an inferior field of study to their own – as when the historian Grote spoke of 'the superior dignity' of historical and scientific truth – and some of them have little or no use for poetry as a source of pleasure and illumination. Famous defenders of poetry like Sidney and Shelley have tried to persuade them that poetry deserves universal recognition as a vehicle of transcendental truth. I happen to believe that this theory of poetry is true, but I shall not try to argue it here.

In contrast with this scientific neutrality, hostility to poetry, whether conscious or unconscious, begins when the critics assume that poems and myths are only peculiar ways of making factual statements. Here is how a standard handbook of Greek mythology presents this view:[1]

> When Spenser personifies the virtue of chastity under the lovely figure of Una, or holiness as the Red Cross Knight, he is merely putting into poetical form what he could have expressed in prose, a current theory, derived from Aristotle, of the virtues and vices, and adorning it with the flowers of his inexhaustible fancy.

In other words, poetry is viewed here as philosophy in fancy dress. One finds a similar attitude in the suggestion by a contemporary historian that myths are 'para-history'. To those who accept the uniqueness of poetry one might as well say that a cat is a para-dog.

In what follows here I call this misguided and misleading

3

approach to poetry – as I see it – 'factualistic'. It differs from the neutral scientific approach in assuming that the primary purpose of poetry is to present factual information and, further, that when poetry fails to present facts correctly it is blame-worthy. This prejudice lies very deep in much of classical criticism. Essentially it is a denial of the validity of poetic imagination and the importance of poetic form.

The worst harm to poetry begins when these factualists not content with misrepresenting the aims of poetry decide to emend it according to their own principles. Classical poetry has been cruelly lacerated by this kind of criticism since the eighteenth century. Richard Bentley's edition of *Paradise Lost* offers an extreme example of factualistic literary revisionism, as will be illustrated later. His basic assumption was that Milton's statements should be scientifically accurate. The result is notoriously absurd. Yet in subtler ways the same factualistic fallacy still pervades many standard editions of classical poetry.

Delusively these factualistic revisionists often profess the highest respect for the poets whose works they mutilate. The nearest analogy that I can find for this hypocrisy is in those smiling fanatics who in the bad old days of religious persecution assured the victims of their rackings and hackings that it was all for the good of their souls. Religious intolerance is happily out of fashion now. Scholastic intolerance lingers on.

In contrast with the enemies of poetry who masquerade as therapists, moralistic critics have been openly and avowedly hostile since the sixth century BC. Taking the opposite view to the factualists, they condemned poets for being irresponsible liars or else for causing immorality by the bad example of the characters they portrayed. The assumption here is utilitarian: poets should make people into better citizens, as Plato insisted. They should be teachers, not entertainers. But the fact is that the greater poets of antiquity, with a few notable exceptions, seldom express moralistic, or didactic, or utilitarian aims – though of course their poems could be used for purposes of that kind. The primary aim of poetry, as implied by many Greek poets and as emphatically asserted by Aristotle in his *Poetics*, is to give pleasure. There is a curious reluctance among classical critics to admit this principle, as if it were an unworthy motive for writing or reading poetry. More must be said about it on a later page.

Moralistic enemies of poetry have often joined in an unholy alliance with politicians to impose partial or total censorship on poetry. Plato and Thomas Bowdler are the chief standard-bearers here, but they lead a large regiment. It may be that in extreme cases, as we shall see, even the most ardent defenders of literary freedom should concede the need for such drastic measures. But only too often these repressive measures have been based on personal prejudice or political partisanship and not on the welfare of society as a whole. Plato in the *Republic* claims to ban poetry for the sake of an ideal society. But at the same time Plato as an ambitious philosopher – and a convert from poetry according to a late source – had strong personal reasons for eliminating the traditional power of the poets.

Other less influential enemies of poetry will emerge on later pages – notably the trivialists who, with Plato, dismiss poetry as 'child's play' or, with Newton, as 'a kind of ingenious nonsense',[2] and the believers in primal stupidity as witnessed in the following remark by Sir James Frazer in the introduction to his edition of Apollodoros:[3]

> By myths I mean mistaken explorations of phenomena, whether of human life or of eternal nature . . . Being founded on ignorance and misapprehension, they are always false, for if true they would cease to be myths.

Here the common factor is an arrogant contempt for the mythopoeic and poetic faculties, in Newton's case resulting from confidence in science, in Frazer's from a nineteenth-century belief in 'progress'. In the present age of disillusion with these optimisms such attitudes are less prevalent. But they are strongly entrenched in the tradition of classical scholarship.

In general, then, this book may serve as a modest reconsideration of the long-lasting dispute between the poets and the philosophers which Plato mentions in his *Republic* – a variety of what Lord Snow has called the conflict of 'the two cultures'. But in the following pages we have to reckon with three conflicting interests rather than two. The scientists seek facts. The moralists seek virtue. The poets and artists seek – to use an old-fashioned term – beauty, that is the effect of artistic excellence on the senses, emotions and mind. These aims are all compatible. If only the three contestants would consistently recognize the integrity and value of the others' approach, there would be no quarrel. My own intention here is ultimately ironical, not polemical – to win wider acceptance of the Aristotelian canon of poetic autonomy and to help to prepare the way for a lasting concordat based on quality and mutual respect.

Specifically in the next four chapters I shall try to reply to the main strictures of revisionists – historical, scientific and philosophical – on poetry. After that I shall consider certain misleading fallacies which have caused even sympathetic critics to misrepresent the poetic art. In writing about these fallacies I was aware that I might myself have been guilty of some of them in my own publications. Perhaps even the present work is not free from them. Indeed one of my basic assumptions here may be fallacious – that the nature of poets and poetry has remained much the same since Homer's time, so that what modern poets have said about themselves and their aims may be also applied to their classical predecessors. Classical literary criticism has recently profited from comparisons between contemporary oral poetry and early Greek epic. I hope that in the same way what we know about the inner thoughts and feelings of poets like Shelley and Tennyson and Yeats may help us to understand more about the undocumented mental processes of Homer and Horace.

It has been suggested to me by some who have been kind enough to read chapters of this book in advance that criticism of past scholars like Bentley and Leaf is rather *vieux jeu* – flogging dead horses, in fact. But Leaf's *Iliad* and some of the other books that I cite are still standard works for students of the classics, and Bentley's extravagances are unparalleled as examples of how far berserk revisionism can go. It would have been easy enough to quote cautionary illustrations from the work of contemporary classicists. But since my aim is to persuade rather than to provoke I have avoided reference to living scholars. If, however, readers come to the conclusion that the hostile views of poetry illustrated here are now obsolete, then the main theme of this book is only an echo from a less enlightened past. For my own part, I do not think that these misunderstandings and misrepresentations of poetry have by any means disappeared. On the contrary, they will always, I fear, be with us – perhaps in new forms, but in essence still antipoetic. If what I have written helps a few students with literary interests to recognize these enemies and their fallacies more clearly than before, I shall be well satisfied.

Chapter Two

Historicists

During the last century and a half many of the worst mis-representations and mutilations of classical poetry have come from those historical scholars and critics who have adopted the factualistic belief that poetry is essentially a sub-species of history – history in fancy dress or primitive history. To isolate these enemies of poetry from historians who fully accept the generic distinctiveness of poetry as asserted by Aristotle, I shall call them 'historicists'. When these historicists go to extremes and proceed to re-write or re-model poetry on their factualistic principles I shall call them 'revisionists'. At that stage they resemble the formidable prospectors in Giraudoux's comedy *La Folle de Paris*, who having discovered rich deposits of oil under Paris are determined to extract it no matter what damage they do to the city. Happily some resolute citizens foil them.

This aggressively historicistic approach must be carefully distinguished from two other attitudes of historians towards poetry and myth. The first of these rests on the principle that creative literature is impenetrable to historical analysis and should never be used as evidence for historical facts. According to this view, as George Grote expressed it,[1] the Greek myths are 'a special product of the imagination and feelings, radically distinct both from history and philosophy: they cannot be broken down and decomposed into the one, nor allegorised into the other . . . We are not warranted in applying to the mythical world the rules either of historical credibility or chronological sequence'.

Against this cautious approach there has always been a

second school of thought which believed that critical methods could at times distinguish fact from fiction in creative literature. Grote described this as 'semi-historical' and dismissed it as 'interpretative guesswork', which 'frittered away the characteristic beauty of the myths into something essentially anti-mythical'. But it continues to be strongly advocated and practised by reputable scholars.

It is not the concern of the present book to consider the relative validity of these historical and semi-historical approaches. That is a matter for historians, not for literary critics. Neither way of thinking is necessarily hostile to poetry, though the semi-historians sometimes merge into semi-historicists by implying an inferior status to their poetic material. I have heard a scholar describe his efforts to find historical evidence in Homer as 'sieving out nuggets of history', the implication being, it seems – to adapt Marlowe's line about Helen – 'All is dross that is not history'. Small regard for John Keats's realms of gold there!

The prime enemies, then, are the doctrinaire historicists. It took over two thousand years of European literary criticism for them to establish themselves in full force. The early Greek historians and their successors were in little danger of treating poetry as a sub-species of history, having been warned in a solemn passage of Hesiod[2] that there were two kinds of poets, those who told the truth and those who told 'falsehoods that look like the truth'. Subsequently Solon had repeated the same warning – 'Poets tell many lies'.[3] The Greeks also were well aware that their early poetry was 'song' and that singers are concerned with artistic effects not factual statements. On the other hand in the absence of non-poetical and non-mythical descriptions of early times they felt compelled to try to pick out firm historical facts from what the poets had sung. Herodotos[4] accepted the historical reality of figures like Heracles and Penelope, but he questioned details in their stories on grounds of common sense. In dealing with Homer's account of Helen of Troy he preferred to trust the Egyptian version which, he claimed, Homer probably knew but altered 'because it was not so suitable for his epic poetry'. Later he again showed his distrust of poetical sources in the phrase 'If one ought to say anything on the evidence of the epic poets'. There is a hint of disparagement in phrases like this – understandably since at that time historians were still finding it hard to persuade their audiences that they deserved to be listened to as much as the poets.

Thucydides[5] also adopted a partly sceptical and partly speculative approach. He rejected 'the story-telling element' (*to muthôdes*) in previous literature. Story-tellers, he warned, habitually wrote to please and Homer being a poet was 'likely to adorn his material with exaggeration' (the 'cosmetic fallacy'). When citing Homer he used such cautionary phrases as 'if Homer is sufficient witness for anyone' and 'if we ought to put trust in the poetry of Homer'. Yet he was prepared to believe in the historicity of Pelops, Heracles, Helen, Achilles and others, and he even accepted, with some reserve, Homer's account of the numbers of the Greeks at Troy. But neither Herodotos nor Thucydides nor any historian since, so far as I know, could establish a valid criterion for distinguishing what looks like fact and what is fact in poetry and myth. This, as Aristotle emphasized a century later, is particularly hard in dealing with a poet like Homer who excels in *paralogismós*,[6] the art of giving verisimilitude to fictions. Undeniably poets sometimes use facts as poetic material, as modern archaeology has proved in the case of a few objects described by Homer. But, as Aristotle warns, one must not conclude that because one fact in a statement is true, any of the rest is true. An anecdote about Samuel Johnson[7] illustrates this common-sense attitude. In a conversation about a scholar whose works 'though full of interesting topics' were 'unhappily found to be very fabulous', a friend suggested, 'Suppose we believe *half* of what he tells.' Johnson replied, 'Ay, but we don't know *which* half to believe.' When Boswell asked, 'May we not take it as amusing fiction?', Johnson answered, 'Sir, the misfortune is, that you will insensibly believe as much of it as you incline to believe.'

Plato, being a brilliant myth-maker himself, thoroughly

understood how perilous it is to rely on plausible myths as evidence for history. Echoing the words of Hesiod, Socrates remarks in the *Republic*:[8] 'In the case of myths, too . . . since we don't know the truth about ancient times, we can make the falsehood (*pseúdos*) like the truth, and so make it useful'. And when Socrates is asked in the *Phaidros* whether he believes in a rationalistic interpretation of a myth he says that such speculations are a futile waste of time: so far as he is concerned it seems best to accept the conventional way of looking at myths.

It was Aristotle in his *Poetics* who voiced the most powerful protest in antiquity against treating poetry as if it were history in verse. At the outset of his great treatise[9] he asserted that it was not the function of poetry to state facts about individuals as history does. Poetry generalizes. It does not describe actual personages like Alcibiades, but presents a *mimesis* (I shall return to this word later) of what people like Alcibiades might do or say. (Later on Aristotle ironically concedes that a poet may *sometimes* state facts if they suit his poetic aims.) Then he enunciates that dictum which has caused so much heart-burning among historians – 'Therefore poetry is more worthy of respect and more philosophical than *historia*.' (The fact that Aristotle has just referred to a historical person, Alcibiades, seems to imply that he primarily means 'history', not 'scientific enquiry' in its broader sense.)

This is a most remarkable tribute to the intellectual value of poetry, and all the more remarkable because it comes from a scientist. Whatever historians may think about the attitude implied towards *historia*, undeniably it made two positive and authoritative affirmations: first that poetry, far from deserving the contempt former philosophers had shown towards it, deserved the highest respect, and secondly that its nature was entirely different from what the factualists tended to think.

Paradoxically, however, in his historical writings Aristotle sometimes drew on mythological sources for evidence. He could hardly have done otherwise if he wanted to write about the remote past at all. It is curious, all the same, that he could ignore his own warnings against the deceptive powers of poetry. 'Homer', he had provocatively asserted in the *Poetics*,[10] 'has taught the other poets how to tell falsehoods as a poet should.' Strange, then, to use poetry as historical evidence.

The problem continued to concern historians from the fourth century onwards. Ephoros[11] warned against the illusions and incantations of the poets and observed that 'in the case of events long ago we hold that those who go into details are the least to be believed, since we consider it highly improbable that the actions and words of men should be remembered for so long.' Polybios declared that the time was past for quoting poets and mythographers as witnesses to disputed facts. Genuine lovers of learning, he claimed, would find the truth in history, but only deceptions and emotions in poetry. But he also tried to rationalize the myths to make historical sense. A few, like Diodoros and Pausanias, were more willing to accept them literally. Meanwhile critical writers on mythology, like Euhemeros and Palaiphatos (*On Incredible Things*) worked hard to reduce mythical marvels to factual possibilities, in the manner of the earlier allegorists but with a greater show of scientific plausibility. Some of their suggestions are not unlike modern sociological interpretations, as when Palaiphatos explains that the story of how Actaion was torn to pieces by his own hounds really refers to an Arcadian youth who neglected his lands for love of hunting, and so his fortune was consumed by his hounds. Other mythographers explained Scylla as a beautiful courtesan, Atlas as a great astronomer, the Chimaera as a fierce queen who had two brothers called Leo and Drako. Here rationalization has turned into creative fiction.

The same variation in attitude can be observed among the Roman historians. Livy was careful to distinguish between 'uncontaminated records of deeds actually done' and 'poetic tales', though once again no clear borderline was established. When for want of other evidence he recounted the legendary stories of early Italy he cautiously qualified them with phrases like 'it is generally agreed' or 'they say'. In general, the Romans being inclined to pragmatism rather than to philosophy considered both history and poetry as subsidiary to oratory and rhetoric – luxuries rather than necessities of public life – and rhetoricians being artists in words and concerned with persuasion rather than information tend to find poetry more instructive than prose. Quintilian went so far as to describe history as a kind of poetry free from metre.[12]

Among later Greek writers Lucian in his essay 'How to Write History' insisted on the mutual independence of poetry and history, though he also recognized their interdependence. The poet must be conceded absolute authority and freedom in his own domain. If one tries to extract facts from his fictions, one must make full allowance for the poet's absolute freedom to alter and invent. While historians are not permitted even the most trifling falsehood, a poet has only one law – his poetic intentions. When inspired by the Muses he can portray such wonders as horses able to talk or to run on water or over the ears of a cornfield without bending them. As Lucian saw the literary scene of his own time, history was more threatened by poetry than the reverse. In fact when history was used for flattery or propaganda – as the risk was under the Roman emperors – it turned into a kind of 'prose poetry'.

In the Middle Ages there was even less inclination to impose factualism on poems and myths than in the later classical period. Scientific history and historical science yielded to pietistic and fabulistic writings. The supernatural mattered more than the natural, the allegorical than the literal, the visionary than the observational, all of which was very much in favour of poetic freedom. During the renaissance the general veneration enjoyed by the great poets of antiquity prevented efforts to treat them as anything but supreme masters of an autonomous art. George Chapman's almost idolatrous reverence for the Homeric poems as fountains of transcendental wisdom proved how far this awestruck approach could go. A strong reaction was bound to follow, and with it came the full doctrinaire historicism.

One can see this new movement well on its way in the third edition of Giambattista Vico's *Scienza Nuova* in 1744. Vico rejected the renaissance veneration of the *Iliad* and *Odyssey* as 'a conscious effort of profound philosophy'. The philosophers, he asserted, did not find their philosophies already embodied in Homer, they themselves inserted them there. Then having effectively exposed one fallacy, Vico proceeded to substitute another to suit his historical interests. Homer, he proclaimed, was 'the first historian of the whole gentile world'. The Homeric poems are 'civil histories of ancient Greek customs'. The early Greek myths can be converted into sound history by allegorical interpretation. For example, the transformation of Cadmus into a serpent could denote the origin of the authority of aristocratic senates.

Vico also described the Homeric poems as 'the mirror of a simple age' and decried some of its episodes as having been 'born of the clumsiness of the heroic minds'. Here we see an early instance of an assumption, common among historians, that the intellects of the ancient poets were unquestionably inferior to their own. This self-indulgent belief in 'primeval stupidity', *Urdummheit*, is a modern innovation. (It is not the same as Eratosthenes' opinion that Homer was ignorant of much that came to be known later, for ignorance of facts is not simplicity or clumsiness.) I shall look at this 'primitivistic fallacy' again on a later page.

Other features of Vico's approach to Homer are curiously contradictory. On the one hand after an erudite survey of the internal and external evidence for the existence of a person called Homer he concluded that, like the Trojan war, he was a fiction, just an 'idea' or else 'a heroic character of Grecian men in so far as they told their history in song'. His reason presumably was that it suited his historicistic approach to minimize the element of interference by a living poet in writings which Vico regarded as imperfect historical documents. (We shall see how Gilbert Murray argued the same kind of theory in his *Rise of the Greek Epic*.) On the other hand elsewhere in his *Scienza* Vico talks, like an enthusiastic renaissance man, of Homer as 'the father and prince of sublime poets'. This ability to dehumanize Homer on one page and to eulogize him as a genius on another often recurs in historicistic criticism.

In the later eighteenth and early nineteenth century the advance of historical studies established ancient history as the salient area in classical scholarship. History in general, which had been regarded in late antiquity and in the Middle Ages as an appanage of rhetoric, now became an empire in itself. Friedrich Wolf in his *Prolegomena* of 1795 asserted that the right method of investigating the Homeric poems was strictly historical: 'Our whole enquiry is *historical and critical*, not about *the desirable thing*, but about *what actually happened. The arts are to be loved, but history is to be revered:* "Tota quaestio nostra *historica et critica* est, non de *optabile* re, sed de re *facta* . . . *Amandae sunt artes, at reverenda est historia*".' (The italics are Wolf's.) No reasonable literary critic should object to a declaration of loyalty of that kind so long as it is not also a declaration of war on poetry. The historical approach to poems as constituting in themselves a kind of historical document is, of course, valid and valuable. But Wolf's proclamation amounted to a declaration of war on the autonomy and integrity of the Homeric poems. Historical methods, he implied, could discover both the truth about Homer and the truth in Homer. And we may note in passing how Wolf subscribed to the historicist contempt for fiction in the phrase *insipientia mythica*.

Two divergent results followed from this aggressive historicism. On the one hand scholars began to treat the Homeric poems as primitive historical documents dating from different periods – 'the Homeric problem'. On the other, historians became more sceptical about the use of myths and early poems as historical evidence. In Britain at the beginning of the nineteenth century historians such as Gillies and Mitford had freely relied on such sources. But soon (under the influence of German scholars) George Grote, as has already been noticed, repudiated this approach. He expressed his view forcefully in an article written before he published his *History of Greece*:[13]

> That there is more or less of matter of fact among these ancient legends, we do not at all doubt. But if it be there, it is there by accident, because it happened to fall in with the purpose of the mythopoeic narrator, who will take

fact, as he takes fiction, when it is suggested by the impulse in his own mind, or germane to the sentiments of his hearers. To discriminate the fact from the fiction, is a problem which we ourselves know not how to solve, in the absence of some positive evidence independent of the legend itself. We shall gratefully listen, if any one will teach us: but sure we are that some road must be discovered very far removed from that hitherto trodden by historical critics. For we cannot protest too strongly against the process of picking out pretended matter of fact, by simply decomposing the legend and eliminating all that is high-coloured, or impressive, or miraculous; it condemns us to all the tameness and insipidity of prose, but we remain as far as ever from the certainty and solid nourishment of truth.

This return to the Aristotelian principle of an essential difference between poetry and history might have become the dominant doctrine among classical historians if Schliemann had not made his spectacular archaeological discoveries in the 1870s. Historicists now became more confident that Homer was a would-be historical writer. But in fact Schliemann, who himself fully recognized the essentially poetic nature of the Homeric poems, did not prove this historicistic thesis that Homer's intention was primarily to record facts. All Schliemann succeeded in proving was that if you take the *Iliad* as a topographical guide you may unearth places and objects that to some extent resemble its descriptions. (But he failed to reach his first goal – the palace of Odysseus in Ithaca.) In making his equations he was in fact doing the opposite of what the historicists did: he was trying to find archaeological evidence corresponding to Homer's descriptions rather than Homeric descriptions corresponding to archaeological evidence. He excavated Ithaca, Troy and Mycenae for Homer's sake, not Homer for Troy's sake.

Stimulated by Schliemann's triumphs, historicists reached the height of their influence in the latter part of the nineteenth century. As the chief exemplar of this phase I propose to cite Leaf's justly celebrated commentary on the *Iliad*. Though its second edition appeared over seventy years ago, it remains the standard edition in English for students and scholars – a regrettable state of affairs for those who value Homer's poetry as poetry. Yet all of us must be grateful to Leaf for much sound scholarship and, at times, perceptive literary insight. It is the general historicistic tone that, to my mind, is to be deeply deplored.

Leaf states on the second page of his introduction that the Homeric poems 'profess a close acquaintance with the topography of Greece', and that they are also to be taken as 'professing to depict the prae-Dorian age', with 'traces of apparent anachronism'. If by 'profess' Leaf had meant only that Homer pretends to depict a world that existed in the past, no one who believes in the essentially poetic nature of the *Iliad* and *Odyssey* has any reason to demur. Such a view gives no basis for historicistic revisionism. But it is clear from what Leaf says later that he means much more than that: Homer's aim is to give a factual record of a specific period of past history. This, as I hope now to show, is a travesty of Homer's poetic intentions as implied in the poems themselves.

Homer being a particularly unself-assertive poet, we cannot expect any plain statements about his artistic aims. But we can, I believe, make reasonable deductions about them from three parts of his work – the opening words of each poem, his invocations of the Muses, and, rather more speculatively, from his descriptions of other professional bards.[14] The first words of the *Iliad* state its subject plainly – 'the destructive wrath of Achilles'. This is a psychological and ethical theme, not historical. Homer's concern here, like that of all the greater classical poets, is with human nature not with recording the events of the past or future. The scenes, actions and events described in the Troad are subservient to the psychological theme. Man – idealized man – is the measure of all things here as much as in the philosophy of Protagoras. Above all, as the last phrase in the exordium of the *Iliad* states, 'The will of Zeus was accomplished'. One may call that a theological theme, but it certainly is not historical.

The beginning of the *Odyssey* professes a similarly ethical and psychological subject – a versatile man who battled his way home through many hardships and perils. The emphasis here is more biographical than in the *Iliad*. But once again the whole tenor of the poem is humanistic with touches of theology. Perhaps in the background here as well as in the *Iliad* there are glimpses of 'the prae-Dorian age'. But so far as the crucial first words of each poem testify they are certainly not the poet's primary concern.

Homer's invocations of the Muses are more ambiguous, but their implication is, I believe, similar. In the first line of the *Iliad* Homer asks the Muse to 'sing the destructive wrath of Achilles'. This implies that what the Muse provides is to some extent prefabricated – not just a plain information but material that is already in poetic form. In other invocations in the *Iliad* and *Odyssey* the poet asks to be 'told' about various themes. Here the emphasis is on the need for poetic material without any suggestion that it should first be poetically processed. These two attitudes correspond, as will be seen later, to what modern poets have said about inspiration. Sometimes it takes the form of poetic phrases round which the rest of the poem is built. Sometimes it comes as ideas, scenes and images which have to be worded to fit the requirements of poetic form.

The invocation to the Muses that comes before the so-called 'Catalogue' in *Iliad* II has often been quoted in support of the historicistic view. (We may note in passing how historicists have reduced this finely written interlude to the status of a mere 'army list' or 'muster-roll'. As I read it, it is a finely resonant litany of place-names and choice descriptive epithets together with personal details about various Achaeans, such as the memorable glimpse of Nireus, most beautiful of the Greeks after Achilles, 'but a weakling'.) This is the invocation:

> Tell me now Muses who dwell in Olympos – for you are omnipresent and omniscient, while we only hear rumour and know nothing at all, tell me, who were the leaders and lords of the Greeks. For even if I had ten tongues and ten mouths and an unbreakable voice and a heart of bronze, I could not tell or name the mass of them, unless

the Olympian Muses, daughters of aegis-bearing Zeus made mention [*mnesaíath*', not 'remind' here, as Leaf agrees] of as many as went to Troy.

Leaf in commenting on this passage does not refer to the poet's clear confession of ignorance – a confession which is fatal to any theory that Homer claimed personal knowledge of the Mycenaean period. Instead he asserts that the Muses are 'goddesses of Memory', quoting in support a highly improbable derivation of their name from the root of the Greek words for memory. He also notes that they were called 'daughters of Memory' in an early source (that is, in Hesiod but not in Homer: other early Greek poets make them daughters of Heaven and Earth). Therefore, he implies, when Homer invokes the Muses in that way he is using a picturesque expression for 'Well, let me try to remember what actually happened.' The Muse 'tells the poet the history which he has to relate', is how Leaf phrases it in his note on the invocation of the Muse at the beginning of the *Iliad*. In modern terms the Muses serve as a kind of information-bank on which poets can draw at will. This seems to me to be as much a travesty of Homer's attitude to poetry as the statement that he professes to describe a specific historical period.

Let us look at the surviving descriptions of the Muses in early epic. They are presented by Homer and Hesiod[15] as being primarily performers and entertainers. On Olympus they sing and dance to delight the gods. Their songs, according to Hesiod, are about 'things that are and shall be and were', and about gods, men and giants. In the last book of the *Odyssey* they come to earth to chant a threnody at the funeral of Achilles. At the beginning of Hesiod's *Theogony* they appear in a vision to 'breathe' a divine voice into the poet so that he may celebrate 'past and future things and the race of the everliving gods'.

What is the main effect of this inspiration? To provide the poet with accurate information about 'things that were'? Not according to Homer or, to some extent, Hesiod. Hesiod in a passage that remarkably contradicts the mnemonic function of

the Muses says that they bring 'a forgetting of evil things and a
rest from anxieties':

> Even if a man has sorrow in his heart and grief to bring
> new trouble to his soul and is in heart-felt dread from
> them, yet when the bard, as servant of the Muses, sings
> about the glories (or famous deeds, *kléea*) of men and
> about the blessed gods . . . he at once forgets his illness of
> spirit and remembers his troubles no more . . .

Similarly when Achilles is portrayed in *Iliad* IX as playing on
the lyre and singing about glorious reputations (or famous
deeds, *kléa*), the purpose and effect is to soothe his angry heart,
not to record historical events. The element of memory no
doubt is there, but it is subordinate to artistic and ethical
intentions. We can see this strictly professional poetic attitude
to events in the past expressed in the remarks by Helen in
Odyssey III and Agamemnon in *Odyssey* XXIV: the sufferings
of heroes provide subjects for song. History is for poetry, not
poetry for history.

Homer's descriptions of what the Muses do for the professional bards of Phaeacia and Ithaca indicate a similarly
unhistoristic attitude. The Muses bestow the gift of 'sweet
song', and at the right moment they give the poet the impetus
to begin his performance. In the case of the Phaeacian bard
they have 'taught' him to sing effectively. For the Ithacan
bard – who describes himself as 'self-taught' – they have
'implanted all kinds of lays in his heart'. Most significantly, the
Muses, we are told, can give the power to describe past events
'as if' one had been present oneself or had heard about them
from someone else.

Here in a passing reference we have an early insight into
what Aristotle, as we have seen, singled out as a salient characteristic of poetry. The primary aim of poets is verisimilitude,
not verity. Poetry is a world of 'make believe', not a world of
factuality. And, as Homer implies, the effect of creating such a
world is to give supreme pleasure, to 'enchant' and 'to charm',
not to instruct and inform. The patronymic of the Ithacan
bard is Terpiades, 'Son of Joy'.

Hesiod clearly recognized this conflict between verisimilitude and verity when at the opening of his *Theogony* he distinguished between poets who sing about things that look like the truth and those who sing the truth. He implies that his poem will be of the second kind. Here, at last, it might seem, we have authentic grounds for factualistic interpretation of poetry. Ironically, however, what Hesiod proceeds to recount is mainly an incredible farrago of monstrous creatures and totally fantastic events. Readers familiar with the plausible introductions to modern fantasies will not be surprised at this. The more an author insists on the factuality of his story, the more we may expect sheer fiction.

If what has been said in the previous paragraphs gives a fair picture of the early attitudes to poetic inspiration, Leaf's assertion that the Muses are essentially goddesses of Memory can hardly be sustained. On the other hand no defender of poetry need object to Hesiod's description of them as 'daughters of Memory'. There is always likely to be some element of memory in the process of poetic composition. But daughters are not expected to be identical with or even closely similar to their mothers either in life or literature. Hesiod was using a well-thought-out personification. The Muses owe their mother the material for their songs and dances so far as past events are concerned. But they are not content to pass it on to gods and men like children repeating lessons by rote. Their role is to transform memory into art and entertainment and to enable poets to perform a similar role. At the highest level the Muses personified the mysterious power of what in modern times we call the creative imagination. At a lower level they offered an explanation as to how poets could claim to possess detailed information about events that had happened long ago (or, when their poetry was prophetic, about future events). In short they provided both originality and credibility.

I do not, and cannot, claim that this interpretation of the function of the Muses is irrefutably established by the scanty evidence. I offer it only as a more probable view than that of Leaf and other historicists. Unfortunately the classical poets have left us no revealing descriptions of what they experienced when inspiration came to them. On the other hand the Greek critics from the fifth century onwards took an interest in the extraordinary phenomenon, as they saw it, of poetic inspiration. They refused to regard it as a product of memory. Instead, Democritos' theory that it was a form of madness, a divine 'possession', was widely adopted.[16] Plato accepted it in his *Ion*,[17] and Aristotle repeated it both in the *Poetics* and the *Rhetoric*. According to this view, poets in the state of inspiration were like the Corybantic dancers and the ecstatic votaries of Dionysos and the women who received the oracles of Apollo at Delphi – under the control of a supernatural power which deprived them temporarily of their normal mentality. Other critics minimized this irrational element in poetry and emphasized the post-inspirational stages of 'polishing', *ars*, that is, rather than *ingenium*, *techné* rather than *mania*. But none denied the belief that genuine poetry depended on something more than an ability to collect material and put it into poetic form.

Modern poets have generally concurred with their view, as will be illustrated in a later chapter. Inspiration, as they describe it, is an irrational and uncontrollable experience, though it can be encouraged by various stimulants and processes[18] – Housman's glass of beer at luncheon followed by a solitary walk in the country, or Schiller's smelling rotten apples, or Addison's promenade up and down a long gallery with a glass of wine at each end. In our own time the Muses have entirely left the poetic scene, giving way to an equally inscrutable entity, the Unconscious. As E. M. Forster has expressed it,[19] 'In the creative state a man is taken out of himself. He lets down as it were a bucket into his unconscious and draws up something which is normally beyond his reach. He mixes this thing with his normal experiences, and out of the mixture makes his work of art . . .' That something is clearly not a temporarily forgotten fact. Whatever it is, it is the product of mysterious blendings and fusions with the other contents of the unconscious, like the dreams of ordinary people or feverish hallucinations. (But dreams and hallucinations are only like the material of a poem, not its final form, unless we are poets and dream poetry like Coleridge in his *Kubla Khan.*)

Imagination is, of course, the other word for this creative . process – imagination which, in the words of Shakespeare's Theseus in *A Midsummer-Night's Dream,* 'bodies forth/The forms of things unknown' (from which, in turn, the poet's pen 'gives to airy nothing/A local habitation and a name').[20] But the classical critics almost entirely neglected the concept of the creative imagination. As long as their doctrines of the Muses or poetic madness prevailed there was no great need for it. The ideas, images, feelings and sensations which came to the poets in moments of inspiration could be satisfactorily explained as coming from a divine source, externally if it was the Muses, internally if it was a kind of madness.

Just as historicists are strongly inclined to reduce the function of the Muses to a matter of memory so they generally feel it necessary to minimize the power of poetic imagination when they are trying to treat poems as evidence for history. Their hope is that at least some nuggets of history will not have been transformed by the alchemy of the poetic process. We can see this attitude clearly exemplified in Leaf's preface. As a scholar living within a generation of Coleridge's epoch-making theory of imagination he could hardly have ignored it completely as an element in poetry. So he mentions it incidentally: 'There can be no question that, at least in great part, they [the Homeric poems] merely bring back in imagination the "good old days" which have passed away'. (We may note in passing the typical 'there can be no question' and 'merely' here.) But from what Leaf goes on to say it is clear that what he means by imagination is the power to bring vivid pictures to the mind, the low-level *phantasia* of the classical critics, not a free creative power. Homer's only choice, he thinks, was between reproducing 'the real circumstances of the old time' or else 'only' clothing the old tales 'with the garb' of his own days. He makes no allowance for the power of the creative imagination to transform historical facts into pure fiction.

A later passage shows just how closely Homer's liberty to invent and innovate was restricted as Leaf saw it:

> The whole scenery of the poems, the details of armour, palaces, decorations, must have been so long the subjects of song before the Dorian invasion that they had become stereotyped and formed a foundation which the Epic poet dared not intentionally sap, easily though he slipped from time to time into involuntary anachronism.

'Stereotyped . . . a foundation which the Epic poet dared not intentionally sap'. Could any assertion be more alien to the essence of poetic genius and poetic art – genius whose characteristic is to produce entirely new concepts, and art whose function is to transform material into a finer and more pleasing form? To Leaf Homer is the slave of a purely hypothetical set of fixed historical traditions, except when, poor incompetent story-teller, he slips into involuntary anachronism. One may contrast what Homer makes Odysseus say at the end of his long narrative in *Odyssey* XII, 'Hateful it is to me to re-tell things that have already been clearly told'. What poet ever won lasting fame by dealing in stereotypes? But obviously belief in the prevalence of such fossilized facts is basic for historicistic interpretations.

Since Homer's poems are the product of what is still largely a dark age in Greek history, we cannot test Leaf's theory about their unsappable historical foundations on any matter of major importance – as for example whether Agamemnon was any more historical than King Arthur or the Wizard of Oz. But against Leaf's theory of poetic 'dared not', we can set the plain lesson of what poets have dared to do with established tradition in better attested times. Aeschylus and Pindar felt free to place the death of Agamemnon in two different cities, both in contradiction to Homer's location at Mycenae. Schiller presented Joan of Arc as dying heroically on the field instead of being burnt at the stake; he also created an entirely unhistorical meeting between Elizabeth I and Mary Queen of Scots in his *Maria Stuart*. Lucan, an epic poet like Homer, offers some choice non-stereotypes, though his poem was written within a century of the events involved. To suit his poetical and rhetorical purposes he brings Cicero to Pharsalos and invents an eloquent speech for him there. He makes Brutus try to assassinate Caesar before the battle. He asserts that Pompey's second consulate was his first. Topographically he does not hesitate to give grandeur to the Rubicon by placing its source in the Alps. He puts Pelion north of Ossa, the Red Sea in the Persian Gulf, and Pharsalos beside Philippi. Where were the unsappable foundations of history and geography there? And where are the unsappable foundations of fact in other epics like the *Song of Roland*?[21]

One could fill many pages with further examples of indisputable alterations of facts to suit an author's artistic aims and ideals. I add only one more to show how even what seems like a plain and trustworthy statement of fact by a creative writer speaking as a personal eye-witness may be a total fiction. The novelist Graham Greene once described how he had observed 'a look of savage stupidity' on the face of Field-Marshal Earl Haig when Haig was acting as a pall-bearer at Kipling's funeral. Haig died in 1928, Kipling in 1936. Somehow Greene's imagination had invented this vivid dramatic *aperçu*, and then he had come to believe it to be a fact. In Aristotle's terms he was presenting things as they should be artistically, not as they were.

Leaf uses another historicistic figure of speech which also, to my mind, misrepresents the poetic process. He talks, as many Homeric analysts still do, of various 'strata' in the *Iliad*. This was not a new metaphor. Grote had used it cautiously before him. But it gained special potency in the age of spectacular archaeological discovery (though archaeologists have generally followed Schliemann in rejecting the factualistic fallacy and respecting the autonomy of poetry). Its suggestion that poetry, even if worked over and amplified by a series of authors, resembles a stratified site with discrete layers is misleading. Any intelligent adapter – whether one calls him editor, expansionist, interpolator, diasceuast or rhapsode – is bound to blend his new material into the existing poem as imperceptibly as possible if he wants his version to be accepted as authentic. This is quite a different process from the laying down of successive layers by accidental accretion. Poetry is made by fusion and fluxion not by simple addition. If one wants an archaeological analogy for interpolations in the Homeric poems as the analysts see them, the nearest I can think of is the deliberate disturbance of a site in order to provide bogus archaeological evidence.

Those assumptions – that Homer 'professes' a quasi-historical purpose, that he is bound by stereotypes, and that a poem, even when frequently re-edited, resembles a stratified site – are the fundamental axioms of Leaf's *Iliad* as I read it. Though at times, like other historicists, he pays tribute to flashes of poetic genius, in general he shows the traditional *de haut en bas* attitude of the convinced historicist. To take one example. Vico, as we have seen, took the view that the early poets were simple-minded and naive. Leaf in his note on a magnificent scene in *Iliad* XIX readily assumes the same. The poet is describing how the women in Achilles' tent while ostensibly mourning for Patroclos were in fact mourning for their own sorrows. Leaf quotes with evident approval Heyne's remark, *Acumen a poeta nostro alienum*, 'Too subtle for our poet'. In other words we must assume that 'our poet' – whether he was a man called Homer or a Third Expansionist or whoever – could not have had the understanding of the human heart that nine-teenth-century scholars had, sunk as he was in *Urdummheit*. Again one must ask what evidence is there that any poet in Greece, whether pre-Dorian or Ionian or Athenian or anything else, was necessarily less intelligent about matters of that kind than modern scholars?

Combined with such disparagements of the poets of the *Iliad* as psychologists, all through Leaf's commentary there are scathing strictures on the parts which he wishes to condemn as late additions. Passages and phrases are described as 'chaotic', 'awkward', 'untimely', 'inappropriate', 'curiously infelicitous', 'entirely lacking in real artistic unity'. He calls the Battle of the Gods in Book XXI 'a ridiculous harlequinade' and tries to seal that as a final and irrevocable judgment by adding: 'To attribute such work to any of the older poets of the Epos is to deny the possibility of any rational criticism in the field'. (This kind of scholastic intimidation – if you don't agree with our strictures on Homer you're a crass idiot – is a regular feature of historicism. Lachmann had set a high standard in his remark that anyone who failed to feel a difference in spirit between four parts of *Iliad* XI–XV 'will do well not to trouble himself any more either with my criticisms or with epic poetry'.)

Enough, I hope, has now been quoted from Leaf's *Iliad* to indicate how the historicistic position can misrepresent the aims and ideals of poetry. Its general effect on any young student primarily interested in literature as literature and eager to understand and enjoy the *Iliad* as a work of art can only be confusing and discouraging. Plato defined the worst possible psychological condition of any human being as 'division in the *psyché*' (*stásis psuchés*). I can conceive of no more potent instrument for causing such a division as a presentation of such a literary masterpiece in terms of an alien genre. Students who hope to hear the song of the Muses are told to concern themselves with stereotypes and strata.

To pass on from Leaf: towards the end of the nineteenth century a newly developed field of investigation began to influence classical studies – anthropology. With it came further misrepresentations of the function of fiction and poetry, as already exemplified in Sir James Frazer's dismissal of myths as 'mistaken explorations of phenomena . . . founded on ignorance and misapprehension'. In face of such an attitude it is ironical to observe how some of these anthropologists invented a new mythology of their own for ancient Greece, with matriarchs, totems, taboos and a figure entirely unrecorded in Greek literature, the Eniautos Daimon.

Among the young scholars who were temporarily swept off their feet by the new anthropology was Gilbert Murray. We can see the regrettable results in the first edition of his widely read *Rise of the Greek Epic*.[22] Though Murray was by nature a sensitive and sympathetic interpreter of Greek poetry, yet in this early work he readily accepted the historicistic and revisionistic principles of Leaf, combining them with some of the more extreme views of the classical anthropologists. He also introduced a new criterion into Homeric criticism – the concept of 'progress' which was so popular in Britain before the First World War. But he defined progress in a highly unmaterialistic way as 'some movement towards the attainment of that "chief end of man" which is, according to the definition of the Scottish "Shorter Catechism", "to glorify God and enjoy him for ever".' This kind of progress, Murray claimed, could be seen in the development of the Homeric poems. He insisted that the function of poetry was moralistic. The 'test of its value' was 'Does it help to make better men?'

Partly as a result of these melioristic and pietistic theories and partly under anthropological influences Murray advanced his theory of extensive expurgations in the Homeric poems. 'The reforming Homeric spirit', we are told, deliberately avoided mentioning 'primitive' elements like taboos, fertility rituals, human sacrifice and so on, and also 'certain forms of sexual irregularity', in the interests of progress and morality. There is obviously some truth in this. Poets usually select their material – in so far as their material does not select them, as will be suggested later – to suit their poetic intentions. But is there any evidence whatever that Homer's intentions were so pious and progressive? Besides, it is misleading to talk of 'expurgation' except from an established literary corpus, and nothing of the kind is available previous to the Homeric poems themselves. The picture of a succession of Bowdleridai gradually cleaning up successive versions of the Troy Tale is neither attractive nor convincing.

Despite the expurgatory progress, Murray claims to have detected some 'primitive' elements in the *Iliad*. Thersites, we are told, was a *pharmakos*-figure – 'a purgative sacrifice to cleanse the community'. (How many far-fetched theories have been devised to explain the uniqueness of that vivid character – so unepic, so unheroic, so rude, so demagogic, and so worthy of Homer's inventive genius!) Achilles is 'typically and almost without qualification a pure tribal hero'; Agamemnon 'is a tribal hero or divinity'; Diomedes 'seems to be a tribal god or hero' – and so on. Here we have stereotypes in another form, and Homer is strained and stretched by procrustean methods to fit them.

Murray shows himself to have been a thorough-going historicist when he began to write this influential book. 'The first business of all these ancient poets was to record history': 'The *Iliad* was meant for history or what then stood for history'. As a historicist he is committed to denigration of the Homeric poems. He must prove that acute critics cannot accept them as well-composed unified structures. So if any readers more interested in poetry than in history or anthropology have their hopes raised by the title of one chapter, 'The Iliad as a Great Poem', they will have a saddening experience. Murray asks, 'Why is it that the *Iliad* is a good poem when it has so many of the characteristics of a bad one?' (Note that he asks 'why' and not 'how', and 'great' has now become 'good'.) He gives his reasons for its badness: its subject is second-rate; its language is loose; its descriptions are 'ready-made' and they 'show a lack of originality and even of sincerity'; several similes are out of place; the battle scenes will 'not bear thinking out'; the phrasing is often obscure, ambiguous, or inept. All this helps to prove that the *Iliad* is 'a traditional book', Murray believes.

In the later part of his book Murray moves away from this kind of historicism towards literary appreciation. Immediately after his list of faults – and after an unconvincing effort to argue that a poet can be 'original' without offering much that is 'novel', an important point for historicists – he asserts:

> Intensity of imagination is the important thing. It is intensity of imagination that makes a poet's work 'real', as we say . . . And I suspect that ultimately the greatness of a poem or work of imaginative art depends mostly on two questions: how strongly we feel ourselves transported to this new world, and what sort of a world it is when we get there, how great or interesting or beautiful.

Transported to this *new* world! How can such a concept be reconciled with all the preceding historicism? 'The whole poem', Murray adds, 'is shot through' with symbols of fire, which are emblems of 'a fiery intensity of imagination'. On the last page Homer's name is at last released from sceptical inverted commas, and even the most ardent lover of poetry may be inclined to forgive all when they read about 'that splendid and careless gleam by means of which Homer was accustomed to set all themes in the world aglow', and how 'Homer's poetry was so easy, the sympathy was so clear, the imagination was roused so instinctively, that we must leave it with a sigh'. But then they will remember that Plato used equally affectionate language about Homer when he banished him from his ideal State.

All in all, Murray's gently and beautifully phrased book offers a fascinating document for the study of academic ambivalence. Most of it expounds the pure doctrine of revision-istic historicism. The rest speaks with the voice of a sensitively perceptive and sympathetic lover of poetry. Yet there is so much tortuous self-contradiction involved in this alternation between the two attitudes that the book contributes more to critical confusion than to literary enlightenment. Murray's more mature work was unambiguously on the side of poetry.

Historicism in an even more extreme form is exemplified in a book by another young scholar strongly influenced by anthropological theories – J. A. K. Thomson. Among Thomson's conclusions are:[23] Odysseus is 'an Eniautos Daimon who has become a Hero'; he is also 'a double of Autolykos, who again is a double of Hermes'; 'the story of the Odyssey is the history, not of a man, but of a divinity'; 'Analysis makes it reasonably certain that Penelope originally was a Water-fowl divinity' (the main argument for this absurdity is an alleged identity between the name Penelopeia and *penélops*, 'a parti-coloured duck' – an egregious example of the 'etymological fallacy'). Further, 'the human relation in which Penelope stands to Telemachos undoubtedly represents the relation of the Mother Goddess of the Anatolian type to the subordinate male divinity constantly appearing at her side as son or consort or lover – Telemachos or Adonis or Hippolytos'.

Viewed in the light of the long history of Homeric exegesis this kind of fantasy most resembles the excesses of the allegorists. It relies on the same mixture of improbable etymologies and of even less probable linkings of fragmentary evidence. Thomson himself involuntarily provided a comment on all such fanciful theories: 'The simple audacity of the Greek imagination has something lovable in it, and it has certain obvious advantages for the student as well.'

Most of this chapter so far has been negative – necessarily so, I believe, when such an oppressive superstructure of historicism has been built over the Homeric poems. In compensation I shall end by referring to one of the best books of constructive Homeric criticism in the present century, C. M. Bowra's *Tradition and Design in the Iliad*, published in 1930. By that time the climate of Homeric criticism had changed enough to encourage a young scholar – Bowra was then thirty-two – to produce a work that challenged the fundamental axioms of the historicists. As the title implied, Bowra was primarily concerned with the question of how much was new and how much derivative in the *Iliad*. What matters first of all, he held, is the poem not the poet and his historical background. He could even dare to say on his first page, 'It seems probable that there was a single poet called Homer, who gave the *Iliad* its final shape and artistic unity, but who worked in a traditional style on traditional matter' – a balanced and temperate statement of all that can justifiably be conjectured from the existing evidence.

Bowra made it clear at the outset where his loyalties lay:[24] 'The *Iliad* is a poem and must be treated as such'; 'Out of the traditional material a whole was made, and it can only have been the work of a single creating poet'; 'Homer wrote to please'. The *Iliad*, he accepted, has faults, but they are faults permissible in a long epic poem and can be paralleled from other epic poems. When he came to the question of historicity

Bowra showed a readiness to employ historical evidence wherever it was firmly established or reasonably probable. There might indeed, he believed, have been a 'central fact' round which Homer composed his poem. But the historical existence of personages like Agamemnon, and the historicity of the Trojan War, could be established only by independent records. Nothing entirely conclusive of that kind had been found. Various historical hypotheses 'are only guesses, and the appearance of any new evidence may overthrow them entirely'. 'Poetry is not history, and it is absurd to expect an epic poet to write a chronicle or even to take trouble with his names and details.'

In his final pages Bowra gave good reasons for accepting the authenticity of a single poet of genius named Homer, and for ranking him with Dante, Shakespeare and Milton. Only Shakespeare, he believed, equalled him in range of tone and in the ability to present comedy as well as tragedy. (What a contrast with Leaf's talk of harlequinades and parodies and an *acumen a poeta nostro alienum*!) Ultimately 'the miracle is that out of a perished world, out of old songs and stories, he created something which is entirely true and convincing . . . real men and women, more real indeed than any of those about him, simplified and sublimated by his creative imagination'.

Fortunate were the undergraduates of half a century ago who found healing in Bowra's book for the wounds inflicted on the Homeric poems by the historicists! The present writer is grateful for having been among them.

Chapter Three

Scientists, Psychologists and Mathematicians

In the last chapter I used the term 'historicists' to differentiate between historians who treat poetry as 'para-history' and historians who recognize its unique qualities. A similar distinction can clearly be made among scientists, though I do not like to use so cacophonous a term as 'scientificists' to describe scientific revisionists. These are the critics who believe that poets should be scientifically accurate and are prepared to emend poems to achieve that ideal. On the other hand, as everyone knows, there has often been a friendly and fruitful relationship between scientists and poets. The frontiers between the so-called 'two cultures' have never been entirely closed to peaceful commerce. Master-poets have found inspiring ideas and images in scientific inventions like the telescope and the microscope, and scientists have found delight and solace in poetry. But since the fourth century BC when Zoilos, the 'Scourge of Homer', assailed the Homeric poems on scientific grounds, there have been critics who have refused to grant poetry its autonomous status as defined by that magnanimous scientist Aristotle. It is a strange paradox, in a way, that Aristotle the prosaic empiricist – his one attempt at poetry was hardly a success – should have treated poetry so sympathetically while Plato, the prose-poet and idealist, should have condemned it so totally in his *Republic*. But if the story is true that Plato was suddenly converted from wanting to be a poet,[1] then perhaps we can recognize the proverbial zeal of a convert against his former faith.

In what follows I shall cite extreme cases as the best way of illustrating the worst effects of the factualistic fallacy in the scientific field. I do not wish to imply that poets never make ridiculous mistakes in their references to natural phenomena, or that they should not be criticized for doing so. But I do wish to emphasize Aristotle's judgment that what matters in poetry and art is verisimilitude rather than verity, persuasiveness rather than accuracy, pleasure rather than instruction, and that statements in poetry that are contrary to scientific fact, whether through choice or ignorance, are reprehensible only when they harm the effect of the poem. The unicorns of medieval romance and Achilles' talking horse in the *Iliad* became acceptable to readers if the poet has the power to charm us into the willing suspension of disbelief which all art needs for its success.

The scientist who reads poetry from the factualistic point of view finds two elements objectionable. One is easily exemplified – the objection to statements contrary to verifiable facts such as Coleridge's crescent moon with 'one bright star, Within the nether tip' in his *Ancient Mariner,* or Rider Haggard's description of an eclipse at the time of the new moon. The second source of distrust goes deeper. It results from the profound difference in perception between the scientist and the poet. This can be illustrated by two incidents in the lives of the poets Yeats and Blake. Yeats one evening was taking part in a crystal-gazing séance with a friend who was a scientist.[2] After gazing into the crystal for a while, Yeats said: 'I see a majestic, shining figure waving over an abyss; I see other shapes – scarlet, green, purple, fluttering around'. His scientific friend interrupted him: 'Mr Yeats, you see no such things. What you are looking at is a reflection from the apothecary's shop across the street. If you look out of the window you will see a row of jars filled with coloured water – scarlet, green, purple – and the shining brass fixtures supply the shining figures'. William Blake expressed a similar disregard of normal perception:[3]

> 'What', it will be Question'd, 'When the Sun rises, do you
> not see a round disk of fire somewhat like a Guinea?' O no,

no, I see an Innumerable company of the Heavenly host
crying, 'Holy, Holy, Holy is the Lord God Almighty' ...

Faced by a contrast between these imaginative reactions to
sensations on the one hand and the observations of a scientific
observer on the other, the average person will tend to support
the scientists. The scientists' statements are verifiable. The
poets' could be merely personal delusions or possibly even
deliberate impostures – or, in the terms used by the ancient
critics, poets may be regarded as liars or madmen. Common
sense seems to rule these visionaries out of court so far as
actuality and factuality is concerned. But to judge from the
testimonies of many poets, beginning with Hesiod, these
abnormal perceptions are as actual and factual to them as
normal sensations are to others. It is true that such a degree of
visionary power as Yeats and Blake claimed to have is unusual.
But all genuinely poetic inspiration has, I believe, something
in common with it. Certainly the visions and inspirations of
the poets are as important for literature as the observations of
scientists for science.

In the examples of scientific factualism and revisionism
which follow here it will be evident that arguments from
science and arguments from common sense merge into each
other – naturally, since observational science has been well
defined as organized common sense. But in most cases science
is called in – often by non-scientists – to administer the killing
blow to the poetical statement. Then readers are inclined to
say, 'That settles it: the oracles of science have spoken', even
when they were inclined to grant the poet some poetic licence
beforehand, just as in the medieval period the verdict of
religious dogma was accepted as conclusive against anything
that science might allege.

Besides this difference between the visionary mentality of
poets and the factual mind of scientists, there is another cause
of misunderstanding. The poet often looks for an aesthetic
ideal where the scientist seeks knowledge. Yeats spoke for the
poet in his *Celtic Twilight*:[4] 'If beauty is not a gateway out of the
net we were taken in at our birth, it will not long be beauty,

and we will find it better to sit at home by the fire and fatten a lazy body or to run hither and thither in some foolish sport than to look at the finest show that light and shadow ever made among green leaves.' We may contrast this with the sterner scientific attitude as expressed by a contemporary scientist. Having described the spectacular colour effects that light can produce in certain conditions, he commented:[5]

> These beauties of form and colour, so constantly recurring in the vivid phenomena of refraction, diffraction and interference, are, however, only incidentals; and, though a never-failing source of aesthetic delight, must be resolutely ignored if we would perceive the still higher beauties which appeal to the mind, not directly through the senses, but through the reasoning faculty.

The contrast between the visionary-aesthetic and the scientific attitudes marks the extremes between which many intermediate grades of literature lie. At one end of this spectrum are the genuine poets who try to be scientists, like Lucretius. At the other end are genuine scientists who try to be poets, such as, perhaps, Erasmus Darwin. As in Newton's colour-spectrum – which delighted so many poets – one cannot mark a clear division here at the point where creative poetry yields to empirical science. The ideal, of course, is to combine superb poetry with impeccable scientific accuracy. But the two are ultimately incompatible, I believe. The poet must alter and re-shape his data to suit the exigencies of poetic art, and at the same time must listen to the promptings of inspiration or madness or whatever one calls the essence of poetic genius. The scientist must avoid the artifices of creative literature and the intrusion of irrational feelings if he wants to achieve lucid precision. When the mathematician-fantasist Lewis Carroll sent his illustrator, the eminent artist Tenniel, a photograph of Alice Liddell as a model for the pictures of Alice in *Alice in Wonderland*, Tenniel in reply asked Carroll how he would feel if he were sent a copy of the multiplication tables.[6] (On the other hand Tenniel did not think it artistically inept to give his picture of the lion in the episode of the Lion and the

Unicorn the face of Gladstone the politician. Such are the intricacies of fact and fiction in art!)

A glance at the early history of scientific criticism of poetry may be useful here. The scanty surviving records of the early Ionian philosophers and scientists do not show a special interest in questioning specifically scientific statements in the poets. Hecataios dismissed poetical fictions as 'many and ridiculous'. Xenophanes and others were content to dismiss epic poets as unreliable witnesses and demoralizing falsifiers. In the latter part of the fifth century criticisms in detail began to appear. A certain Hippias, probably the Hippias of Thasos who died under the Thirty, was cited by Aristotle in his *Poetics* as having suggested a slight change in the pronunciation of a Homeric line to avoid a suggestion that oakwood and pinewood rotted easily.[7] Another pre-Aristotelian critic condemned Homer for 'unscientifically' (*anistóreton* is the word used in the scholia[8]) describing the constellation of the Great Bear as being 'alone uncondemned to bathe in the baths of the Ocean', on the grounds that several other northern constellations also in fact are deprived of that kind of bath. (Aristotle resolved the contradiction between poetry and science here by saying that the word for 'alone' is used 'metaphorically' for 'outstandingly, distinctively'.) In the Hellenistic period Eratosthenes repudiated Homer as a reliable witness to scientific facts, but Strabo accepted him as such.

Towards the end of the fifth century poets began to hit back against scientific critics. Aristophanes[9] in *The Clouds* presented the first extant version of a caricature which still recurs in crude comedy, that of the myopic eccentric scientist fiddling with futile experiments. Aristophanes chose Socrates to embody this travesty, quite unjustifiably since Socrates on the whole was hostile to natural science. Socrates and his assistants are ludicrously portrayed as being engaged in grotesque observations and experiments to determine the length of a flea's hop and whether a gnat hums in front or behind. Eventually their Thinking Shop is burnt down to the delight of the populace – as the Luddites in their day tried to destroy the products of nineteenth-century technology. In *The Birds* Aristophanes turned his mockery against Meton the astronomer.

In a later play, *The Frogs*, Aristophanes burlesqued an aspect of literary criticism that specially concerns our present theme. To help in deciding whether the poetry of Aeschylus is better or worse than the poetry of Euripides a pair of weighing-scales is carried in, and the disputant dramatists are asked to speak lines from their plays into the opposite scale-pans – a process described as 'weighing poetry like butcher's meat'. Here the objects of ridicule are not scientists but literary critics and readers who fondly believe that artistic quality can be mechanically quantified. In its cruder forms no sensible person could be deceived by this fallacy. But disguised in the elaborate language of computers it is not unknown in classical criticism.

Also in *The Frogs* Aristophanes briefly pillories another kind of quantitative fallacy, the possibility of measuring poetry with geometrical instruments. Swift exploited a similar idea in Gulliver's voyage to Laputa. Referring to the Laputan scientists, Gulliver remarks: 'If they would . . . praise the beauty of a woman they describe it by rhombs, circles, parallelograms, ellipses and other geometrical figures.' The modern equivalent of this in classical criticism is to be found in exaggerated claims by scholars of finding close analogies between early Greek poetry and Greek geometric vase-painting or pedimental groupings. 'Structure' and 'structuralism' are words of power in contemporary literary criticism, and Aristotle with his insistence on the importance of plot-construction would probably have welcomed them. No one is likely to contend that structural analysis when used with due regard to the fluidity of poetry cannot help towards a better understanding. Nor must one forget how profoundly Greek thought and Greek aesthetics were influenced by mathematics. But at times the elaborate visual schemata proposed as constructional elements in classical poetry go far beyond probability. The fallacy that poetry is speaking painting is involved here. It will be illustrated further on a later page.

In the next generation after Aristophanes the scientific attack on poetry was led by the notorious Zoilos of Amphipolis, nicknamed 'the Scourge of Homer'.[10] He is credited – or discredited – with nine books of criticism of the Homeric poems. The text of this weighty onslaught has not survived, but some of his strictures can be extracted from later sources. He censured Homer for errors in geography, psychology, physics and common sense, objecting, for example, to a simile in *Iliad* XXIII, 100, because it seemed to imply that smoke could descend into the earth. Like Bentley in his edition of Milton's *Paradise Lost*, Zoilos, it seems, adopted a tone of puerile ridicule at times, as when he scornfully asked whether when the Fates of Hector and Achilles were weighed in the scales of Zeus (*Iliad* XXII, 209 ff.) they sat down or stood up in the scale-pans.

Aristotle in his *Poetics* spent a good deal of time in refuting the kind of stricture on poetry that Zoilos produced. In his highly important twenty-fifth chapter he begins by stating the general principle that the subjects of the poetic *mimesis* are not confined to observable phenomena. The poet may present his material in any of three forms – things as they are or were, things as people say or think they are or were, or things as they ought to be. In other words poets may be verists or conventionalists or idealists in presenting their subject-matter. (Aristotle goes on from there to state the all-important principles of poetic autonomy and poetic licence.) Second, poets are entitled to use words either with unusual meanings or else metaphorically. In modern terms, ornithologists are not justified in protesting when Shelley says to his skylark 'Bird thou never wert' or when Keats tells his nightingale 'Thou wast not born for death, immortal bird'. This is poets' language, and if one is going to read poetry one should accept it as readily as one accepts the necessity to speak French in France.

Aristotle recognizes a third reason for failing to understand poetic phrases – language-changes in the meaning of words in the course of time, as in Milton's 'Every shepherd in the vale/Under the hawthorn tells his tale [counts his flock]', and Hamlet's 'I'll make a ghost of him that lets me [prevents me]', and in the traditional collect 'Prevent us O Lord in all our doings [Go before us . . .]'. To ignore the possibility of such changes is as fallacious as to ignore changes in manners and morals, as will be illustrated later.

At times, however, errors of fact in poetry cannot be explained linguistically. In that case, Aristotle observes, the poet may have made a deliberate change in order to suit his poetic purpose, or he may unconsciously have made a mistake. For example when a poem describes a horse as moving in an unrealistic way or a female deer as having horns, the poet is not blameworthy if the alteration or error does not spoil the general artistic effect. In fact, as Aristotle saw it, it is better for a poet to be scientifically inaccurate and poetically effective than scientifically accurate and poetically ineffective.

Aristotle did not mention another possible defence against allegations of palpable misstatement in poetry. But the geographer Strabo did, some three centuries later. (He, in contrast with Eratosthenes, considered Homer to be a sound geographer.) Noting that Homer's description of a landmark near Ithaca did not correspond with what could currently be observed, he suggested that a natural cataclysm might have changed the conformation of the land since Homer's time.[11] Modern scholars have made the similar suggestion that Homer's hot and cold springs near Troy, which have never been satisfactorily located, may have been destroyed in a local earthquake. Such changes are certainly possible in volcanic Greece. If a description of Thera before the great eruption had survived, few might have believed it until modern science established the fact.

But such explanations and defences while they may satisfy factualists like Strabo are irrelevant to the poetic art. If the ghost of Homer were censured in Hades for topographical inexactitude he might well reply as A. E. Housman replied to a similar criticism, when he became aware of a scenic error in his lines:

> The vane on Hughley steeple
> Veers bright, a far-known sign . . .

Housman decided not to correct it. He explained his reason:[12]

> I ascertained by looking down from Wenlock Edge that
> Hughley Church could not have much of a steeple. But as
> I had already composed the poem and could not invent
> another name that sounded so nice, I could only deplore
> that the church at Hughley should follow the bad
> example of the church at Brou, which persists in standing
> on a plain after Matthew Arnold said [in his poem 'The
> Church at Brou'] that it stands among mountains. I
> thought of putting a note that Hughley was only a name,
> but then I thought that would merely disturb the reader.
> I did not apprehend that the faithful would be making
> pilgrimages to these holy places.

Aristotle's magisterial reply to the Zoilan kind of criticism
discouraged further efforts to depreciate poetry on scientifically
factualistic grounds. The Alexandrian editors for the most part
confined their criticisms and emendations to contradictions
and anomalies within the poems themselves. As Porphyry
phrased it,[13] the Aristarchan method was to clarify Homer
from Homer – a sound Aristotelian principle. They did at
times allow current fashions to affect their judgment in matters
of decorum, as will be exemplified later. But they consistently
treated the poems that they edited as poems, not as would-be
factual documents.

Occasionally, however, factualism – or some may say,
common sense – kept breaking in from outside the poetic
context. One ancient commentator on Theocritos took exception to a statement that lions mourned in Sicily at the death
of Daphnis.[14] Pointing out that there was no evidence for the
existence of lions there, he neatly emended the line to mean 'If
there had been lions in Sicily they would have mourned for
Daphnis'. The critical fault here was failure to recognize that
the whole atmosphere of the death of Daphnis as described by
Theocritos was mythological not realistic, unlike the earlier
part of the idyll. The same fault is to be found in one of the few
instances of emendation by a royal patron of scholarship.
Ptolemy II of Egypt, being interested in botany, objected to
Homer's mention of violets and wild celery as growing together

in Calypso's island. To improve botanical probability he emended 'of violet' (*iou*) to 'of marshwort' (*siou*).[15] But goddesses' islands, like the sea-coast of Bohemia, can transcend nature – and who would want marshwort round their home when they could have violets?

During the Middle Ages and the Renaissance science and scientific criticism slumbered while allegory and allegorical interpretation ran wild. A change came in the seventeenth century, primarily as the result of the empirical philosophy of Bacon. The foundation of the Royal Society of London in 1662 and of the Royal Academy of Science in Paris four years later marked the growing influence of the new way of thinking. The new scientists' strictures were not only against the content of poetry – we remember how Newton viewed poetry as 'a kind of ingenious nonsense' – they also objected to its language. Bishop Thomas Sprat in his *History of the Royal Society* (1667)[16] argued that '*eloquence* ought to be banish'd out of all *civil Societies*, as a thing fatal to Peace and good Manners', and with eloquence should go 'specious *Tropes* and *Figures*'. Members of the Royal Society and other persons of scientific bent should, he said, 'reject all the amplifications, digressions, and swellings of style' and should 'return back to the primitive purity, and shortness, when men deliver'd so many *things*, almost in an equal number of *words*'. Later he asserts that '*The Wit of the Fables and Religions* of the *Ancient World* is well-nigh consum'd; They have already serv'd the *Poets* long enough; and it is now high time to dismiss them'. (But 'the *Wit* which is rais'd from *Civil Histories*, and the Customs of *Countries*, is solid and lasting'.) It would be well, Sprat believed, if an English Academy were established as 'a fixt, and *Impartial Court* of *Eloquence*; according to whose Censure, all Books, or Authors, should either stand or fall'. Other reformers of the time suggested similar measures. Bishop Samuel Parker wanted an Act of Parliament to curtail the use of 'fulsom and luscious Metaphors' in sermons.[17] Happily these episcopal scientists were no more successful in their advocacy of literary control then Plato was in his – partly, no doubt, because when the Society set up a committee for improving English it contained John Dryden and John Evelyn.

The effects of the scientific revolution on literary criticism are plainly exemplified in the work of Richard Bentley, perhaps the greatest of English classical scholars. Born in the year of the foundation of the Royal Society, Bentley was strongly influenced by the pervading scientific spirit. His earliest publication to win wide recognition was the initial contribution to a series of lectures endowed by a bequest of Robert Boyle, 'the Father of Chemistry and Brother of the Earl of Cork', which were founded to prove the truths of the Christian religion. In composing them Bentley made extensive use of recent scientific theory and research to support Christian theism, and he discussed some of his arguments with Isaac Newton. When he became Master of Trinity College Cambridge he did much to encourage scientific research in the University.

Bentley's gigantic stature as a scholar needs no emphasis here. His boldness and ingenuity in conjectural emendation have never been surpassed, and in several cases his conjectures have been confirmed by subsequently discovered papyri. Yet, quite astonishingly, he produced an edition of *Paradise Lost* (1732) that is infamous for the crass insensitivity of its 'scientific' alterations in the received text. It rivals the worst excesses of the historicists as an exhibition of anti-poetics. Its faults have often been attributed to senility. This is wrong. Bentley produced a fine edition of Manilius (himself a poetic critic of poetry) seven years later and subsequently began work on editions of both Homer and the New Testament. It seems more as if his previous triumphs as an exposer of frauds and an emender of textual corruptions went to his head for a while with tragi-comic results. Housman judged that as early as 1722 Bentley, when writing his notes on Lucan, 'had acquired the worst habits of deity'.[18]

Showing extraordinary perversity for a scientific critic, Bentley in his preface invented an intermediary between Milton and his printer as a convenient way of explaining the huge number of errors, as he saw them, in the text – or, in Bentley's more vigorous terms, of accounting for 'such miserable deformity' and 'flat nonsense' in it. Bentley added one of those arrogant remarks that we have already met among dogmatic scholars who want to terrorize others from defending poetry: 'Whoever . . . will contend that they are the Poet's own, betrays his Ill Judgment as well as his Ill Nature'. In fact there is as little evidence for the existence of his supposed intermediary as there is for centaurs and chimaeras.

The worst of Bentley's many bad emendations in *Paradise Lost* are notorious. I shall quote only three egregious examples of misplaced reliance on science, logic and prosaic common sense.[19] The first foists on Milton the kind of improvement that Housman as a poet categorically rejected. Commenting on the phrase in the exordium of *Paradise Lost*, 'the secret top of Horeb or of Sinai', Bentley mocks the notion that the peak of a mountain 'visible several leagues off' could be 'secret'. In case the reader should argue that clouds and mist could make a mountain-top secret, he adds, 'I have in my Youth read several Itineraries where the Travellers went up to the Top of Horeb; and I remember not, that they take notice of its Cloudiness'. Besides, Bentley knows 'from Natural History' that 'a mountain whose Head is cloudy, has always running Springs at its Foot', while holy scripture makes it clear that Horeb had none. Further, 'the best Poets have adjudg'd' that 'a Proper Epithet is always preferable to a General one'. So it seems that science and the Bible and the best poets concur with Bentley in deleting 'secret' and inserting 'sacred'.

Are we overwhelmed? No. First, as Bentley knew better than most, *secretus* in Latin often meant 'lonely, solitary, set apart', and Milton revelled in Latinisms. Second, on the factualistic level, it is obvious that a remote and lonely mountain peak would be an excellent place for conveying esoteric illumination. Third and fourth, 'sacred' spoils the assonance with 'seed' in the next line, and reduces the phrase to a platitude (as with so many of Bentley's emendations, such as 'adventurous wing' for 'adventurous song'). Fifth, Bentley's reliance on the distinction between proper and general epithets begs the question.

At times Bentley's mad logic was reminiscent of Lewis

Carroll's characters in the Alice books. (I have suggested elsewhere that Carroll might have had Bentley in mind when portraying Humpty Dumpty with his knock-down argumentation.) For example, Bentley's note on the line

> Thither came Uriel gliding through the Eeven

is:

> I never heard but here, that the *Evening* was a Place or Space to *glide* through. *Evening* implies Time, and he might with equal propriety say, *Came gliding through six a clock.* But it's the Printers' language: the author gave it, Thither came *Uriel*, gliding through the Heav'n.

So sensible, so logical, so scientific, and so wrong in terms of high poetry, or indeed, of textual criticism!

In other examples the reliance on contemporary science as an instrument for lacerating Milton's poetry is more strongly implied. Bentley appeals directly to chemistry, the special subject of his former patron, Robert Boyle, in the note on Milton's opulent list of gems in Book III:

> These nine Lines may be well spar'd, and restor'd to the Editor: who had a mind to shew, he knew the Terms at least of Chymistry. But when among the *Gems* he reckons the *Philosopher's Stone,* as if the Chymists describ'd it literally a *Stone,* his Pedantry and Affectation became insufferable. 'Tis well if he [Satan] can escape with his *Gold* and *Silver* and *Gems* there [near the sun]: the Body of the Sun being justly computed a Million of times hotter than glowing iron, and his Rays at this distance, collected by a Burning Glass, melting every thing in an instant.

The whole nine lines, Bentley decides, should be deleted – insufferable pedantry and affectation indeed! Altogether he deleted over a thousand lines and offered about eight hundred emendations. Subsequent editors have accepted about six of his corrections.

Bentley applied the same standards of scientific matter-of-factness to some of his emendations of Horace, though there, as in other ancient authors, the likelihood of textual corruption gave his talent for detecting real errors greater scope than in

Paradise Lost. Two of his best-known emendations were based on a scientific approach. Horace in his *Epistles*[20] tells a fable about a little fox (*vulpecula*) which slipped in through a chink in a grain-bin, ate the grain, and then found itself too fat to get out. Bentley in his famous edition appeals to the reader to reject the absurdity of a fox here, because a fox does not have the broad, flat teeth necessary to masticate grain. So we must read *nitedula*, 'a dormouse', for *vulpecula*. Many eminent scholars accepted this factualistic emendation. It is generally rejected now.

There is one good and sufficient Aristotelian reason for rejecting it despite the further arguments adduced in the fifteen hundred words or so of Bentley's formidable footnote. Aristotle cautioned critics that poets may portray conventional ideas and not factual things. Horace was most likely paraphrasing a fable by Aesop (mentioned cursorily by Bentley) in which a fox is undeniably the victim of its own folly in eating too much, the moral being that even so clever an animal can be betrayed by greed. Aesop and Horace are not describing fauna as zoologists know them but are writing about an imaginary world where animals can speak to each other and eat whatever suits the fabulist.

Here Bentley's dormouse (did Lewis Carroll find another idea there?) had no support in the manuscripts. But in another famous crux Bentley had the best manuscripts on his side. Horace in one of his *Odes*[21] is describing a rural scene in Italy during a holiday:

> *Festus in pratis vacat otioso*
> *cum bove pagus* [variant reading, *pardus*]:
> (The festive village [leopard] idles with the ox
> Lazy in the meadows . . .)

Against those misguided editors who preferred the leopard to the village Bentley thunders: 'Look here, how did a leopard get into Italy? Their habitat is confined to Africa and Asia . . .' The answer to that is: if, as is arguable, Horace is describing a supernatural visionary scene, like Isaiah in his messianic prophecy and Theocritos in his Daphnis idyll, a leopard as an emblem of Dionysos is poetically as much entitled to be in Italy as Carroll's Jabberwocky in Looking-glass-land. Bentley, however, adds other linguistic arguments which probably establish *pagus* as the right reading.

Horace himself in the opening lines of his *Ars Poetica* gave his view of poetic licence. The poet's descriptions must not, he says, violate probability. But at the same time, 'Painters and poets have always had an equal licence to dare anything'. In his pragmatic Roman way he then comes down more strongly on the side of verisimilitude. As he said later on, 'Let fictions made for the sake of giving pleasure be very close to actuality'. But his problem is how far can a poet go in his imaginary creations without losing credibility among his readers, not whether facts must be adhered to for the sake of factuality.

In the present era of classical criticism scientific factualism is less in fashion. But like influenza and the common cold, it could always break out again in a new form resistant to existing poetic antibiotics. The safest prophylactic is to keep the Aristotelian canons of poetic autonomy always in mind. At the same time scholars should constantly listen to what the poets themselves say about the relationship between poetry and actuality. I offer two cautionary examples. Coleridge, as already mentioned, deliberately altered an astronomically possible feature in his *Ancient Mariner* to an astronomically impossible one. In his earlier version he wrote

> Till clomb above the Eastern bar
> The horned Moon, with one bright Star
> Almost atween the tips.

His final version read

> . . . Within its nether tip.

It has been suggested that here Coleridge was influenced by a publication in the *Philosophical Transactions of the Royal Society* for 1794 entitled 'An Account of an Appearance of Light, like a Star, seen in the dark Part of the Moon . . .' But even if that were so, it is significant that he changed a scientifically possible phenomenon into the entirely obvious impossibility of an actual star nearer to earth than the moon. His main motives, I believe, were poetic: to avoid the awkward 'atween' and to give a more eerie and supernatural air to his spectral seascape.

My second example shows a thoroughbred scientist in confrontation with a master-poet. Charles Babbage, who for ten years was Lucasian Professor of Mathematics at Cambridge, having read or heard Tennyson's lines

> Every minute dies a man,
> Every minute one is born,

observed that on those terms the population of the world would remain static. So he told Tennyson 'I would therefore take the liberty of suggesting that in the next edition of your excellent poem the erroneous calculations to which I refer should be corrected as follows: "Every moment dies a man/And one and a sixteenth is born".'[22] He added that this phrasing was a concession to the exigencies of metre, as the increase was not exactly a sixteenth.

In reply to this accommodating proposal Tennyson, who valued accuracy when consonant with poetry, accepted the vague term 'moment' for 'minute' and altered his lines to

> Every moment dies a man,
> Every moment one is born,

leaving it to further statisticians to argue about what he meant by 'moment'. Very likely what helped him to make the change was the richer euphony embodied in 'moment' rather than 'minute', for as we have seen, the reason why Housman refused to make a similar change for the sake of factual accuracy was that he could think of no equally euphonic alternative. On another occasion Tennyson made a similar change. When someone told him that Mars had moons of its own he altered

> She saw the snowy poles of moonless Mars

to

> She saw the snowy poles and moons of Mars.

When one turns to consider the views of psychologists on poetry one finds a much smaller amount of hostile criticism than the school of Bentley offers. The reason is plain. Natural scientists, physicists and chemists can observe and describe visible events, and state with confidence that leopards were not indigenous in Horace's Italy and that no star can come between the moon and the earth. Psychologists have to deal with unobservable and often unpredictable forces in the human psyche. They can study the products of motivation and imagination and conation and inspiration, but they cannot measure and quantify them as a chemist can quantify the ingredients of an explosive mixture.

On the other hand psychologists, unlike other scientists, are bound to have a professional interest in literature, and literary critics are bound to have an interest in psychology. Both study the same objects – the workings of the mind, heart and senses, and of human nature in general – though their methods and values differ in many ways. As we have seen, Democritos and Plato discussed psychological aspects of poetry. Since that time all critics who concern themselves with problems of poetic inspiration or of characterization within poems have been psychologists to some degree.

But psychologists become enemies of poetry when they make poetic characters and incidents seem nauseating or ridiculous to everyone except dedicated psychologists. Here are a few examples.[23] The Cyclops, we are told, is the 'prenatal nucleus' of the *Odyssey*, his cave being a symbol of the womb. Odysseus is 'the hero who masters castration anxiety'. The Sirens represent a mother's invitation to incest, the mast to which Odysseus is bound being a phallic symbol. Scylla and Charybdis symbolize a choice between succumbing to a breast complex or to an Oedipus complex. The Aeolus incident records failure to adapt to toilet training. The myth of Prometheus shows that 'in order to gain control over fire men had to renounce the homosexually-tinged desire to put it out with a stream of urine'. Caves, groves, arrows, columns, swords, snakes, all take on a Freudian life of their own.

The ingenuity of such interpretations equals that of the early Greek allegorists. But there is an essential difference. The allegorists, with a few lewd exceptions, tried to give poetry higher meanings. More than a few modern psychologists have tried to lower it to the most sordid levels of human behaviour.

It would be foolhardy for a non-mathematician to try to compare the more esoteric features of mathematical thinking with the poetic process. But some of the more remarkable analogies between poetry and pure mathematics must be briefly mentioned here. On the whole mathematicians, in so far as they have adopted any attitudes at all to poetry, have generally been friends rather than enemies, and they have sometimes understood the thought-processes of poets better than most other external observers except musicians. Generally, too, mathematicians have recognized the autonomy of the poets within their own sphere of action.

The first notable similarity between the pure mathematician and the pure poet – by 'pure' here I mean composing formulae and poems which are not subject to what Aristotle called 'things as they are' – is that neither the poet nor the mathematician refrains from thinking and composing in terms of imaginary concepts – winged horses, minotaurs, the square root of minus 1. In Euclid's beautifully satisfying system of geometry we are asked to think in terms of physical impossibilities like points that have position but no magnitude and lines which have extension but no thickness. Such conditions are as foreign to the world of actuality as those in Lewis Carroll's *Through the Looking Glass*. It is true that when mathematicians use terms like 'imaginary' and 'irrational' they have not the same denotations as in literary criticism. (One difference, as a mathematical colleague pointed out to me, is that though the square root of minus 1 is imaginary and the square root of 3 irrational they can be trusted to behave consistently, unlike centaurs and satyrs.) But in essence the terms have a good deal in common.

Second, both poets and mathematicians contrive their compositions on the basis of pattern and symmetry, the mathematicians making their patterns from symbols for ideas, the poet making them out of elements of sound (rhythm, phonetic quality, voice melody) as well as from words for ideas. (The fact that both sounds and ideas are significantly combined in the medium used by the poets makes a poem more complicated in material than a mathematical formula.) Guided and inspired by the instinct for pattern and symmetry both poet and mathematician, when they are original and creative, advance in thought far beyond existing models. Aristotle's insistence on the importance of structure, 'plot', as he called it, in the arrangement of events in drama is applicable to the mathematician's development of his formulae as well as to the poet's arrangement of his ideas.

Third, the aesthetic criterion is active in both disciplines. Mathematicians frequently talk of beauty and elegance as qualities of their formulations. This is because the constituents of these qualities in mathematics are much the same as in poetry and art – symmetry, proportion, balance, economy, all high ideals of the classical aesthetic tradition.

Some quotations from mathematicians will illustrate their attitude to these affinities. In a lecture on astronomy delivered in 1832 Sir William Rowan Hamilton observed:[24]

> Be not surprised that there should exist an analogy, and that not faint nor distant, between the workings of the poetical and of the scientific imagination . . . With all the real differences between Poetry and Science, there exists, notwithstanding, a strong resemblance between them; in the power which both possess to lift the mind beyond the stir of earth, and win it from low-thoughted care; in the enthusiasm which both can inspire, and the fond aspirations after fame which both have a tendency to enkindle; in the magic by which each can transport her votaries into a world of her own creating . . .

Hamilton said much the same in a letter in 1829:

> I believe myself to find in mathematics . . . a formable matter out of which to create Beauty also . . . to my particular constitution of mind, a mathematic theory presents even more of 'the intense unity and energy of a

living spirit' than the work of a poet or of an artist. Even the Principia of Newton, which is ordinarily perused as a model of inductive philosophy, I consider as being rather a work, a fabric, an architectural edifice, the external results of which have been and will be changed by the progress of experimental science, but which will always be interesting to mathematicians as a structure of beautiful thoughts.

Hamilton tried hard to become a good poet as well as a mathematician, but unsuccessfully. His friend Wordsworth's replies to Hamilton's requests for comments on poems were models of gentle tactfulness. But though Hamilton never showed proof of genuine inspiration by the Muses he once fully experienced the thrilling effect of sudden inspiration in his mathematical thought. For a long while he had been trying to find the key formula for his theory of quaternions. His family were aware of his efforts to such a degree that his sons used to ask him anxiously at breakfast whether he had found it yet. Then one day, as he himself described, he was walking with his wife and half-listening to her conversation while 'an under-current of thought' was going on in his mind. Suddenly 'an electric current seemed to close; and a spark flashed forth', and at once he was able to write down the elusive formula. Other mathematicians and scientists have testified to this kind of sudden and involuntary revelation in terms very like those used to describe poetic inspiration.

More recently the Cambridge mathematician G. H. Hardy[25] has also described the similarity between mathematics and poetry, though here one finds a depreciatory tone not to be found in Hamilton's remarks:

> A mathematician, like a painter or a poet, is a maker of patterns. If his patterns are more permanent than theirs, it is because they are made with *ideas*. A painter makes patterns with shapes and colours, a poet with words. A painting may embody an 'idea', but the idea is usually commonplace and unimportant. In poetry ideas count for a good deal more; but, as Housman insisted, the importance of ideas in poetry is habitually exaggerated: 'I cannot satisfy myself that there are any such things as

poetical ideas . . . Poetry is not the thing said but a way
of saying it . . .'

The mathematician's patterns, like the painter's or the
poet's, must be *beautiful*; the ideas, like the colours or the
words, must fit together in a harmonious way. Beauty is
the first test: there is no place in the world for ugly
mathematics . . . It may be very hard to *define* mathematical beauty, but that is just as true of beauty of any
kind – we may not know what we mean by a beautiful
poem, but that does not prevent us from recognizing one
when we read it.

Hardy supports his opinion that the ideas of poetry are on
a lower level than those of mathematics by the lines from
Shakespeare's *Richard II*

Not all the water in the rough rude sea
Can wash the Balme from an anoynted King.

He comments:

Could lines be better, and could ideas be at once more
trite and more false? The poverty of the ideas seems
hardly to affect the beauty of the verbal pattern. A
mathematician, on the other hand, has no material to
work with but ideas, and so his patterns are likely to last
longer, since ideas wear less with time than words.

Here one can catch an echo from Bentley's knock-me-down
style of criticism. It is not demonstrably true that the patterns
and ideas of the *Iliad* or the *Odyssey* or *Macbeth* or *Richard II*
have been less durable, less influential and less original than
those of any mathematician. When Hardy picks out only two
lines from the enormously complex pattern of *Richard II* for
intellectual depreciation, he falls, if I understand him correctly,
into the fallacy of quoting a short phrase, and one voiced by a
dramatic character, out of context and taking it as expressing
the whole of the poet's meaning. Besides, the 'idea' in Shakespeare's lines is not 'salt water won't wash away anointing
unguent', nor is it simply 'the divine right of kings is indelible':
it is also a new association of thought between the sea with all
its physical symbolic qualities and kingship with all its social
and mystical resonances. Yet, apart from professional bias,

Hardy's insight into the essence of poetry is authentic and acute. His emphasis – overemphasis, perhaps – on poetry as a way of saying things rather than a provider of information is valuable. But again one must insist that one cannot divide the substance from the attributes, the word-pattern from the idea, as he does.

The resemblance between mathematics and literary fiction has been emphasized by another scientific writer. Describing how pure mathematics works by a structural process, he observes that this process is[26]

> not quite that of inventing a game, but rather that of the continued invention of a game in the course of playing the game. This kind of game-inventing is akin to the writing of a novel, and the parallel is indeed quite close up to a point. There never was a person called Sherlock Holmes, nor even a person like Sherlock Holmes. Yet his character was well defined by the description of his consistent behaviour in a series of fictitious situations. Once Conan Doyle had composed a few good stories with Sherlock Holmes as their hero, the image of the detective – however absurd in itself – was clearly fixed for the purposes of any further such stories. The main difference between a fictitious mathematical entity . . . and a fantastic character like Sherlock Holmes, lies in the greater hold which the latter has on our imagination. It is due to the far richer sensuous elements entering into the conception of Sherlock Holmes. That is why we acquire an image and not merely a conception of the detective.

This writer shows no inclination to depreciate the fictional image – on the contrary. As it happens, however, his remark that Sherlock Holmes had no prototype in nature is incorrect. Conan Doyle himself stated that his model was a surgeon in Edinburgh, Dr Joseph Bell, who excelled in making deductions about the private lives of his patients – which is a perfect example of Aristotle's maxim: the poet does not describe characters as they are in life, he generalizes their characteristics in new fictional characters.

The reference to the game-element in mathematics recalls, but contrasts with, Plato's depreciation of poetry and art as 'child's play'.[27] Modern anthropologists and psychologists have come to recognize how deeply this element of play affects human life and thoughts, and the concept of *homo ludens* as well as *homo sapiens* is now familiar. The supreme exemplar of the mathematician-gamesplayer was Lewis Carroll (Charles Dodgson). His amazingly imaginative *Through the Looking Glass* depends as closely on a game of chess for its structure as Joyce's *Ulysses* depends on the structure of the *Odyssey*. Carroll doubled the structural complexity of his book by making its second condition that of the reversed image in a mirror. Instead of constricting his imagination, these two structural controls provided a firm and clear runway for the flights of his imagination. Chess-pieces became vivid characters, chess moves became fantastic journeys, and out of the blue came a Jabberwocky, Humpty Dumpty and a host of fantastic creations. The astonishing thing is that Carroll is better remembered by semanticists for Humpty Dumpty's views on words and their meanings than by mathematicians for any of his publications on mathematics.

This paradox, that what was regarded as child's play or nonsense or fantasy in its own day may anticipate later scientific developments, can be seen also in Greek myths. The aeronautical exploits of Daedalus, Icarus and Bellerophon in early myth, and of Trygaios in Aristophanes' *Peace*, are familiar. Problems of extended prolongation of life are implicit in the story of Tithonos. Midas was given the power to transmute metal without any help from physics or chemistry. Changes of sex were experienced by Teiresias, Caineus and Salmacis. Chemical warfare from the air is humorously suggested in Aristophanes' *Frogs*, and a space satellite in his *Birds* (as in Swift's *Voyage to Laputa*). Arion anticipated modern delphinologists. Theseus emulated Jacques Cousteau in undersea exploration. Lucian described a voyage to the moon in his ironically titled *True History*.

These imaginary anticipations were different from those of Jules Verne in the nineteenth century. Verne's orientation was scientific, though his primary aim was to write a good story.

Chapter Four

Philosophers

'The poet always stands in need of something false. When he pretends to lay his foundations of truth, the ornaments of his structure are fictions; his business consists in stimulating our passions, and exciting our prejudices. Truth, exactitude of every kind, is fatal in poetry.' So Jeremy Bentham asserted in *The Rationale of Reward.* He was repeating an opinion that can be traced back to the sixth century BC, when Greek philosophers condemned poets for presenting fictions as truths. As they saw it, to tell falsehoods of that kind was not merely a matter of ignorance and error: it was positively immoral and demoralizing. If we can believe a late source, Pythagoras claimed to have seen a vision of Homer and Hesiod being tortured in Hades for their lies.[1] He gave details: Homer was hung from a tree infested with serpents; Hesiod, tied to a bronze pillar, was emitting shrill shrieks of pain. Heracleitos was a little more merciful.[2] He merely asserted that Homer (and Archilochos) deserved to be flogged.

Before I go on to consider the climax of this attack on the falsehood of poetry which was reached in Plato's *Republic,* a difficulty in terminology has to be met. The regular Greek word for the non-truths of poetry was *pseúdea,* as in Solon's assertion: 'Poets tell many *pseúdea.*'[3] The word and its cognates range in meaning from 'lies' in the strongest sense of that word to 'falsehoods' and 'fictions'. That is to say, these terms can imply a malicious intent to deceive, or an unconscious untruth, or a palpable fiction. The Romans distinguished these shades of meaning more carefully, using *mendacia* for deliberate lies, *falsa* for untruths and *ficta* for imaginative inventions. (Perhaps the Romans were justified in regarding the Greeks as being more prone to lying than themselves, as expressed in Juvenal's phrase *Graecia mendax*. But it is ironical that an example of Greek mendacity quoted by Juvenal,[4] Xerxes' canal through the isthmus of Athos, is a historical fact.)

The ambiguity in the term *pseúdea* makes it difficult to be sure about the meaning of the earliest reference to poetic fiction by a Greek writer. The reference comes in Hesiod's account in his *Theogony* of how he saw a vision of the Muses on Mount Helicon. They told him, Hesiod says,[5]

> We know the way to tell many *pseúdea* that look like
> > factual things.
> We also know, whenever we wish, to utter truthful
> > sayings.

If *pseúdea* here means 'lies', then it would appear that Hesiod was condemning poetry different from his own. But if it means 'fictions', Hesiod's contrast would merely imply that there are two kinds of poetry, one imaginative, the other factual.

In what follows here I shall generally use the word 'fiction' for *pseúdea*, though often in the philosophers' denunciations of poetry it could have all the force of 'lies'. When Plato, with astonishing audacity in face of his condemnation of poetic *pseúdea*, asserted that politicians were entitled to tell a *gennaîon pseûdos* for the sake of the State he is more likely to have meant 'a bold (or noble) fiction' than 'a bold (or noble) lie'.[6]

The attacks by philosophers on poetic fictions provoked a specious defence. It offers a good example of how one fallacy can be adopted as an argument against another fallacy. It emerged in the second half of the sixth century, when two early defenders of Homer's poetry, Theagenes of Rhegium and Pherecydes of Syros, tried to defend Homer from charges of mendacity by arguing that his descriptions of divine misconduct were allegories of physical interactions between the elements, earth, air, fire and water, or else allegories of emotions like love, hate, wisdom and folly. This was manifestly improbable, and the more intelligent Greek critics repudiated it.

Socrates in the *Phaidros*[7] said that rationalizations of that kind were a waste of time, preferring to accept myths in the conventional way, and Plato ignores them elsewhere – and so, too, Aristotle. But the Stoics and Neoplatonists revelled in them, as did medieval and renaissance readers and scholars. Allegory is clearly not a valid method of exegesis for most poets, including Homer. Yet it still continues to operate, often disguised now as anthropology or psychology or in some other modern dress.

The doctrine that poets are liars, or, in milder terms, purveyors of deceptive fictions, found its strongest and most influential advocate in the Socrates of Plato's *Republic*. His basic argument was the same as that of the Ionian philosophers. But he supplemented it and gave it a metaphysical dimension in his famous 'imitation (*mimesis*) of an imitation' doctrine which reduces poetry to a mere copy of phenomena and relegates it, with painting, to the lowest position in the ascending scale towards divine truth, even below carpenters' tables.[8]

This extreme view was not consistently held by Plato. Elsewhere in the *Republic* Socrates suggested a different attitude to art: it could combine various parts of existing things to make a new entity; it could portray non-existent persons; it could even 'imitate' a divine model. In other dialogues Plato recognized the poet's function of organizing material into an organic whole, like a living creature. (In Xenophon's *Memorabilia*,[9] Socrates similarly conceded that an artist could be selective and could express the nature of a person's *psyché* by facial expression and bodily posture.) But these more liberal views have had much less influence on modern classical criticism than Socrates' severe doctrine of second-degree imitation in the *Republic*, which is a belief that admirably suits the factualistic fallacy, since it assumes that poems are mere descriptions of external objects.

Up to now in this chapter I have used the conventional translation, 'imitation', of the Greek term *mimesis*. But, as all students of European literary criticism are aware, mimesis is a desperately protean term. In Plato's mimesis-of-a-mimesis doctrine it can hardly mean more than mere 'copying, making a facsimile of', as when a forger counterfeits a banknote. Earlier in the *Republic* Plato used it to mean 'impersonation', as when an actor plays a part. Here there is no question of substitution: the mimesis and its object remain clearly distinguishable. Further still from mere copying is the meaning implied in the phrase attributed to the Pythagoreans, 'Things are *mimémata* of numbers.'[10] In this last usage all physical resemblance between the product of the process of mimesis and their objects has disappeared. There are many other subtleties of meaning in the term. Literary criticism since Plato has been much confused by its ambiguities, and all kinds of theories have sheltered behind it and its conventional equivalent in English, 'imitation'. But at least when one uses the term 'mimesis' one is giving a warning of complexities and perplexities. By using 'imitation' one can slip in derogatory associations much more easily.

There were two main defences against Plato's derogatory theory of poetic and artistic mimesis, according to whether one believed in the existence of the Celestial Forms or not. As Aristotle did not believe in them, he ignored the question of the relationship between poetry and 'reality' and concerned himself in his *Poetics* only with its relationship with observable phenomena. He ignored Plato's absurd suggestion that poets wrote about inert objects like tables and chairs. Instead, he asserted that the proper subject-matter for the poetic and artistic mimesis (which cannot mean 'copying' here) is 'people doing things' – which, if we include the gods, accurately describes the subject of almost all classical Greek poetry. Further, and essentially, the poet does not try to make his mimesis – 're-presentation' seems to be the best rendering here, though some scholars reject it – from actual personages like Alcibiades in the way in which a historian or a scientist would describe them. The poet abstracts from his knowledge of persons like Alcibiades – brilliant, high-spirited, vain, ostentatious, versatile and unreliable: but Aristotle regarded him as an exemplar of 'the high-spirited man' – *megalópsuchos* – and makes his mimesis from these abstractions and generalizations.

An anecdote from modern times illustrates this process of creation by abstraction. Robert Louis Stevenson on reading George Meredith's novel, *The Egoist*, said to him, 'Now, Meredith, own up – you have drawn Sir Willoughby Patterne from *me*!' Meredith replied with a laugh. 'No, no, my dear fellow, I've taken him from all of us, but principally from myself.'[11]

Aristotle's method of explaining the non-imitative nature of poetry was essentially a matter of logic. As he saw it, a poet composed the thought-content of his poems much as a Euclidean geometer composed his theorems. Euclid's elegant and clear-cut propositions are not about specific triangles and quadrilaterals, but about types of figures – not about any diagram that could be drawn on a board or in sand, but about ideal figures in which the lines have extension but no thickness and the surfaces are perfect planes. Out of these abstractions and generalizations Euclid constructed theorems that have been studied for over two thousand years. The same is true of poets. By generalizing and universalizing from specific objects they make theorems of permanent interest and worth. If the poet merely 'copied' Alcibiades or a table, his poem would have value as material for history, but only trifling value in itself. Poetry is like architecture, adapting its materials for its own special purpose. It is not a process of reproduction. In non-artistic matters everyone prefers the original to a copy. The more mimetic the art is, the more it approaches non-art. When King Agesilaos of Sparta was invited to hear a man who imitated a nightingale amazingly well, he declined on the grounds that he had heard nightingales themselves singing. Keats's 'Ode to a Nightingale' cannot justifiably be ignored for that reason.

I have extended Aristotle's answer to Plato much further than his brief statement in the *Poetics* goes. But those seem to me to be its implications in terms of the modern attitude to representationalism in art and literature. On the other hand Aristotle had nothing to say about purely abstract or imaginary art. He emphasized that a large part of the pleasure of poetry and art consisted in identifying the products of mimesis with their subjects if one knows them personally, as in identifying a portrait-painting. This is true even of highly imaginative modern poetry. Keats's 'Nightingale' has its links with an actual English nightingale as well as with the bird of myth and symbolism. Wordsworth's poem about the daffodils on the lakeside is probably partly autobiographical and descriptive. But it is not a direct mimesis of anything except the poet's own thoughts and feelings.[12]

Those who were willing to believe in Plato's Heavenly Ideas could offer a different defence of poetry against the charge that it is a mere copy of sensory phenomena. This defence is implicit in the famous passage in Cicero's *Orator* where he is talking about the sublime work of Pheidias:[13]

> Nor did he, when he formed Jupiter or Minerva, have before his eyes a model which he followed strictly, but in his own mind he had an extraordinary idea of beauty. This he contemplated, on this he fixed his attention, and to the rendering of this he directed his art and his hand ... These forms of things Plato calls ideas ... and these, he maintains, do not arise occasionally in our minds, but are permanently present in our reason and intelligence.

It recurs in the fifth book of Plotinos' *Enneads*:

> the arts are not to be slighted on the ground that they produce their creations by imitation of natural objects ... We must recognize that they give no mere reproduction of the thing seen, but go back to the Reason-Principle from which Nature itself derives. Much of their work is all their own. They are containers of beauty and add supplements where nature is deficient. Thus Pheidias made his Zeus according to no model from among the things of the senses, but by apprehending what form Zeus would have to take if he chose to become visible.

Applied specifically to poetry, this transcendental theory of poetic truth became the creed of many poets and critics in the renaissance period and later, as evidenced in Sidney's and Shelley's defences of poetry. Plainly it can neither be proved or disproved, based as it is on a metaphysical hypothesis.

There was another way for critics of poetry to express the belief that poetry was imitative – the doctrine that the function of poetry was to offer a mirror-image of life and nature, which Plato alludes to briefly in the *Republic*. One finds it first in a casual metaphor in Pindar's seventh *Nemean Ode*.[14] It recurred again in a remark by the fifth-century sophist Alcidamas when he pronounced that the *Odyssey* was 'a beautiful mirror of human life'.[15] It is not clear what precisely he meant. Did he mean, in a factualistic sense, that the *Odyssey* recorded the actual experiences of an actual person? But if so, what about fantastic monsters like Scylla and Charybdis and the Cyclops? What did they mirror? More likely, perhaps, Alcidamas meant that the *Odyssey* allegorically reflected the trials, temptations and triumphs of Everyman, as the Stoics and Cynics understood it. Whatever he meant, his metaphor became a cliché in subsequent criticism. I have heard a good classical scholar quote it recently in defence of a historicistic position.

Before I follow this mirror-image of poetry further,[16] it should be recalled that the mirrors of antiquity, being made of polished metal, not of mercury-backed glass, gave a much less perfect reflection than ours today. In fact 'as in a mirror' was used by some classical writers as a simile for 'misleading, deceptive, unclear', the best known example being found in Saint Paul's chapter on Love in I Corinthians 13: 'Here we see in a mirror, enigmatically, there [in heaven] face to face'. Alcidamas could have meant something of that kind in comparing the *Odyssey* to a mirror: it reflected human life not precisely and in clear detail, but enigmatically.

The most famous use of the comparison among English-speakers came some two thousand years after Alcidamas. Hamlet in the second scene with the Players says that the aim of acting 'both at first and now, was and is, to hold, as 'twere, the mirror up to nature'.[17] The important thing to note here – besides the cautious 'as 'twere' – is that Hamlet was not referring to the poetic art at all. He was telling actors, not poets, what to do. And even they, he went on to imply, should not be mere mimics, for they should 'show virtue her own feature, scorn her own image, and the very age and body of the time his form and presence' – which comes close to Aristotle's theory of poetic generalization.

Emphatically, then, in this often quoted line Hamlet was not referring to the poetic art. If one wants to find in Shakespeare a description of what poets, as distinct from actors do, it comes in Theseus' speech in *A Midsummer-Night's Dream*:[18]

> The poet's eye, in a fine frenzy rolling
> Doth glance from heaven to earth, from earth to heaven;
> And, as imagination bodies forth
> The forms of things unknown, the poet's pen
> Turns them to shapes, and gives to airy nothing
> A local habitation and a name.

It is true that this assertion is made in one of Shakespeare's more imaginative plays, not in a historical one. It is also true that the light-hearted phrase 'airy nothing' would not suit the material of *Julius Caesar* or *Coriolanus*. But it is arguable that even in plays of that kind poetic 'madness' and imagination are essential. I shall return to these themes shortly.

The mirror theory of poetry appealed to the rationalistic mood of the eighteenth century. Samuel Johnson pronounced in his *Preface to Shakespeare*:

> Shakespeare is above all writers, at least above all modern writers, the poet of Nature; the poet that holds up to his readers a faithful mirror of manners and life.

But how can a mirror reflect abstractions like manners and life? A mirror reproduces individual objects, not general concepts. Johnson repeated the metaphor, and at the same time rejected the doctrine of poetic madness, in another passage:

> This therefore is the praise of Shakespeare, that his drama is the mirror of life; that he who has mazed his imagination in following the phantoms which other writers raise up before him, may here be cured of his delirious ecstasies, by reading human sentiments in human language, by scenes from which a hermit may estimate the transactions of the world, and a confessor predict the progress of his passions.

Aristotle's reply to that would probably be that while Shakespeare in his more naturalistic plays gives a greater appearance of actuality by a skilful use of *paralogismós* than many other writers do – but what about Caliban and Puck and Ariel and the rest? – his Hamlets and Lears are essentially as much abstractions as Frankenstein's monster.

The prestige of this mirror metaphor was such – or, those who disagree with me may say, its truth was so cogent – that even so ardent a Neoplatonist as Shelley could use it in *A Defence of Poetry*:

> The drama, so long as it continues to express poetry, is a prismatic and many-sided mirror, which collects the brightest rays of human nature and divides and reproduces them . . . and touches them with majesty and beauty, and multiplies all that it reflects, and endows it with the power of propagating its like wherever it may fall.

There, however, the mirror has acquired such magical properties that factualism has no foothold in it.

To return from this distorting hall of mirrors to Theseus' non-imitative theory of poetry in *A Midsummer-Night's Dream*: it combines two further arguments against the Platonic doctrine of slavish imitation. The key words are 'frenzy' and 'imagination'. Poetic madness had a long history, back to the philosopher Democritos in the fifth and early fourth century BC. He, living in a rationalistic age, tried to find a physiological explanation of poetic inspiration instead of the traditional reference to the Muses. Democritos had observed, apparently, that, in certain states, mad people uttered unpredictable and extraordinary things similar to poetry in its more imaginative forms. So he suggested that the source of poetic inspiration was not an external voice, but an internal prompting. 'Whatever a poet writes with *enthousiasmós* and with holy in-breathing (*hieron pneûma*)', he asserted, 'is especially beautiful.'[19] *Enthousiasmós* – literally 'the condition of having a god inside one' – was regularly observable in Democritos' time in the mediumistic state of the Pythian priestess at Delphi when delivering her oracles, as well as in some everyday kinds of madness. 'Holy in-breathing' – a phrase that can be traced back to Hesiod's *Theogony* – has obvious similarities with the Christian doctrine of the Holy Spirit, especially in its pentecostal aspects.

Some scholars have interpreted this seminal pronouncement about poetic madness as referring only to the more ecstatic kinds of Greek poetry, like the dithyramb. But in another fragment Democritos implied that even a comparatively sane poet like Homer needed this divine possession to produce his 'beautiful and wise verses'. Later critics from Plato to Cicero and Horace took the same view that all genuine poets needed it. Plato stated categorically in his *Phaidros*:[20]

> Whoever comes to the gates of poetry without the madness of the Muses in the belief that technical skill will make him a competent poet, fails. The poetry of a sane man vanishes in the presence of the poetry of madmen.

On this basis he went on to hint that poets in their ecstasy might catch glimpses of the Divine Realities – in contradiction to his mimesis-of-a-mimesis doctrine.

Aristotle referred to poetic madness very briefly in his *Poetics*.[21] Being interested there only in matters that were amenable to observation and rational analysis, he did not try to probe this mystery. He contented himself with asserting that a true poet must either have a high degree of natural ability to adapt himself to other characters (*euphués, eúplastos*) or else be capable of entering a state of ecstatic madness (*manikós, ekstatikós*). Some editorial enemies of irrationality have tried to emend this reference to madness out of Aristotle's text, unconvincingly. Bywater, being eager, apparently, to minimize the importance of poetic madness, translated *manikós* as 'with a touch of madness in him'. There's no mere 'touch' in the Greek.

Obviously both kinds of poet, the madman and the man of 'plastic' talents, have existed in all epochs of literature. Some poets, like Shakespeare, combined both. Sometimes he used the poet's frenzied eye. Sometimes, as Coleridge remarks in his *Biographia Literaria*,[22] he entered into the natures of his characters and yet remained himself, changing his shape, as it were, but not his identity like Proteus in the *Odyssey*. As examples of the more ecstatic kind of poet one can point to Aeschylus, Coleridge and Yeats (who, according to his friend Gogarty, used to compose 'with great mental agony': 'With his hands behind his back, his head down or suddenly looking up, he would pace the floor humming and murmuring to himself until the poem arose from the rich darkness.').[23] On the 'euplastic' side are Sophocles, Virgil and Pope. But none of them would have been master-poets if they had not combined genius with artistry, *ingenium* with *ars*.

At times poets past and present have deliberately tried to induce the necessary state of madness or ecstasy by artificial means. Aeschylus and his contemporary Cratinos, the comic dramatist, were said to have composed while drunk, and a phrase of Archilochos may imply the same condition. In modern times poets have tried to find ecstasy in more sophisticated drugs than alcohol. Ralph Waldo Emerson commented on this search for aids to inspiration in his essay *The Poets*:

> The poet knows that he speaks adequately then only when he speaks somewhat wildly, or 'with the flower of the mind'; not with the intellect used as an organ, but with the intellect released from all service and suffered to take its direction from its celestial life; or as the ancients were wont to express themselves, not with intellect alone but with the intellect inebriated by nectar.
>
> As the traveller who has lost his way throws his reins on his horse's neck and trusts to the instinct of the animal to find his road, so much we do with the divine animal who carries us through this world. For if in any manner we can stimulate this instinct, new passages are opened for us into nature; the mind flows into and through things hardest and highest, and the metamorphosis is possible. This is the reason why bards love wine, mead, narcotics, coffee, tea, opium, the fumes of sandalwood and tobacco, or whatever other procurers of animal exhilaration . . .

Whatever interpretation we take of the terms involved in the classical doctrine of poetic madness, it clearly stands against the belief that poetry is essentially imitative. It could be used, as by Plato, to depreciate the worth of poets to be taken seriously – mere ravings. Or it could be used to claim a divine source for poetry, as by Pindar in his phrase taken from oracular procedure, 'Prophesy, Muse, and I shall be your interpreter'.[24] In times when the Bible was a familiar book it helped to give the poet the prestige of a Hebraic prophet, and when Ossianic and druidic lore became popular it emerged in the image of a long-bearded ecstatic bard pouring out prophecies and invectives from a craggy rock.

The reference to imagination in Theseus' speech about the poet points to another defence against the imitative theory of poetry. Its Latin equivalent *imaginatio* was a translation of the Greek term *phantasia* which also produced our terms – frequently used pejoratively – 'fantasy' and 'fancy'. The Greek term was often used for visual imagery derived from the memory, with no implication of creative power. Aristotle did not mention it at all in his *Poetics*, presumably because he did not consider it an important concept for poetic theory. But elsewhere in scattered references he suggested ideas that quite closely approached Coleridge's elaborate doctrine of the creative imagination.[25]

Aristotle distinguished between two kinds of *phantasia*, one, a residual or revived sense-perception, a reproduction of images of actual phenomena which had been stored in the memory, the other, a faculty that could produce images which never existed previously in the mind or outside it. These latter images, he suggested, could result from a process akin to dreaming or to what happens when clouds take strange shapes in the sky. In contrast, the other kind of *phantasia* is rational and logical. In it the mind reconstructs and schematizes sense-impressions as a scientist does with his data. The comparison between the processes of poetic composition and of dreaming became a commonplace of literary criticism, sometimes in appreciation of poetry's unique qualities, sometimes in depreciation. But on the whole the general concept of the creative imagination was ignored until the nineteenth century, and the

misleading doctrine of mimesis prevailed. The notable exception is in Philostratos' life of Apollonius where he remarks in
a discussion on Greek sculpture that *phantasía* is a wiser and
subtler craftsman (or creator, *demiourgós*) than *mímesis* because
mímesis can reproduce only what it has seen but *phantasía* can
produce what it has not seen.[26]

It was Coleridge who established the concept of the creative
imagination as a central critical criterion. His distinction
between 'fancy', by which existing phenomena are consciously
re-arranged, and the full imagination which unconsciously
'dissolves, diffuses, dissipates in order to recreate' has been
modified by subsequent critics. They have suggested that
these two are more likely to be two degrees of the same faculty
rather than separate faculties. As it has been phrased, 'Working
at high tension, the imaginative energy assimilates and trans-
mutes; keyed low, the same energy aggregates and yokes
together those images which, at its highest pitch, it merges
indissolubly into one'.[27] Yet, whatever way one explains this
creative faculty, it stands in direct contradiction to imitative
theories.

In this chapter it has been necessary to touch on several
concepts that have constantly provoked critical discussion and
argumentation, and most of them are by their nature ultimately
inexplicable. What is most significant for the theme of the
present book is that no matter how much one questions the
foundations of the refutations offered by Democritans, Aristo-
telians, Neoplatonists and others to the imitative theory of
poetry, at all events they all are denials of the factualistic
fallacy. Democritos denied it in physiological terms: the poet
raves like a madman. Aristotle denied it in terms of logic:
the poet generalizes, presenting types not individuals. The
Neoplatonists denied it in transcendental terms: the poet rises
above the phenomena of nature. Believers in the creative
imagination denied it in psychological terms: the poet draws
his inspiration from what Henry James called 'the deep well
of unconscious cerebration'. What all these theorists – and
many others beyond mention here – were affirming was:

Chapter Five

Politicians and Moralists

The enemies of poetry described in the previous chapters were mostly concerned with the relationship between poetry and its subject-matter. Politicians and moralists are more interested in the effect of poetry on its audiences. Their fallacy is not factualistic but utilitarian. They believe that the primary function of poetry is to improve people's characters by instruction and example. Those who feel strongly on this sometimes take the view that when poets fail to reach acceptable standards of morality in their work, they should be censored or exiled. As I shall admit later, there may be times when drastic measures of that kind may be justifiable, but only in extreme cases.

Defenders of poetry against moralistic attacks often accept this utilitarian principle and believe that poetry's highest value is educational. The Homeric poems have been presented in that way from early times. A scholar of the present time has gone so far as to assert that Homer composed his poems 'not as a piece of creative fiction but as a compilation of inherited lore'.[1] But Homer never suggests that his aim is didactic or moralistic, though at times his characters make moralistic remarks. He himself implies that the main function of poetry is to give pleasure – sensuous, emotional and intellectual pleasure. It is true, of course, that much can be learned about good and evil, justice and injustice, anger and patience, kindness and cruelty from his poems – witness Archbishop Fénelon's use of Telemachos as an exemplar of princely virtue for the Dauphin of France. Still, there is a clear difference between writing specifically for didactic and moralistic reasons and writing in a way that lends itself to such uses. As Goethe said in his *Dichtung und Wahrheit*, 'A good work of art can certainly have moral effects, but moral aims on the artist's part make him spoil his work'.[2] This can be plainly seen in poems like Wordsworth's *Ecclesiastical Sonnets*.

A few didactic poems of the classical period succeed in being genuine poetry, notably Hesiod's *Theogony* and *Works*, Lucretius' *De Natura Rerum* and Virgil's *Georgics*. The imaginative genius and the technical dexterity of their authors redeems them from prosiness except in their most technical parts. Other didactic poets of antiquity – such as Parmenides, Empedocles, Nicander, Oppian and Manilius – are read only by specialists now. Aristotle in his *Poetics*[3] denies Empedocles the title of a poet, as having nothing in common with Homer except his metre.

Hesiod, though purposefully didactic in much of his poetry, did not condemn poets who wrote pleasing fictions. He recognized, as we have seen, that the Muses sometimes produced plausible falsehoods as well as factual truths. The first Greek to denounce poetic fictions was a politician, if we can trust a late anecdote. When Solon of Athens heard that the dramatist Thespis was arousing great popular interest by his plays, he went to see a performance for himself. Afterwards he asked Thespis was he not ashamed to tell such big lies (or to present such elaborate fictions – *telikaûta pseudómenos*) in front of so many people. Thespis replied that it was not outrageous (*deinón*) to do so as an entertainment (or in a spirit of play, *metà paidiás*). Then Solon struck the ground with his staff and said, 'Well, let me tell you, if we praise and honour that kind of entertainment, we'll soon find it affecting our business contracts.'[4] In other words, if people came to accept impersonations by actors in the theatre, the basis of legal identity would be undermined. If citizen X when performing as an actor was believed to be, say, Agamemnon at Troy, where would such alibis and aliases stop? (In another version of the same story Solon went on to blame Thespis for the impostures perpetrated by Peisistratos in his attempt to win control of Athens.) There is also a statement by a late writer that Solon actually banned Thespis from producing tragedies. But it is likely that we should have heard more about that if it were true.

The first sure evidence for political and moralistic interference with literary freedom comes from Herodotos,[5] who records that Cleisthenes of Sicyon (in the early sixth century) banned the contests of the epic rhapsodists because the epics praised Argos and the Argives so much. Herodotos also describes an act of censorship in Athens a century or so later. In 494 BC the tragedian Phrynichos produced his *Capture of Miletos* before an Athenian audience. The Persians' recent sack of that great Ionian city, closely linked to Athens by kinship, alliance and tradition, had deeply shocked the Athenians. When the disaster was re-enacted with all the emotive power of music, rhythm, dancing, mournful gestures and sorrowful speech-intonations the effect was overwhelming. Herodotos brusquely tells us, 'The audience fell into lamentation.' The intensity of the psychological disturbance apparently was such that the magistrates saw danger to public order. They fined the dramatist 1,000 drachmas and prohibited any further performance of the play. Later in the same century the comic dramatists incurred censorship by their outspoken abuse of prominent personages. A law was passed prohibiting excessively scurrilous remarks about citizens in the public performances of comedies. It seems to have had little effect. A similar law enacted in Syracuse in 415 BC was equally transient. We shall come later to Plato's decree of banishment against almost all poets.

The doctrine that the best poets are, and should be, teachers – and teachers of good morals as well as of useful facts – is first stated emphatically in extant European literature by a character in the *Frogs* of Aristophanes.[6] There Aeschylus at the beginning of his attack on the plays of Euripides gets agreement from his rival that poets should be admired for 'dexterity and for good advice and because we make citizens better people'. Aeschylus goes on to describe how various early poets benefited mankind, Orpheus teaching religious rites and abstention from killing; Mousaios, oracles and cures of diseases; Hesiod, agriculture; and 'divine Homer', military formations, deeds of valour, and armings. Aeschylus then accuses Euripides of practising the opposite of this beneficial didacticism by causing women to commit adultery or to kill themselves in imitation of the love-sick heroines in his plays. (It is a curious fact of history that several suicides apparently resulted from the publication of Goethe's *Werther*: in subsequent editions Goethe inserted a warning to his readers not to follow his hero in that respect.[7])

Euripides tries to defend himself by pointing out that the story of Phaedra was known before he used it for his play. Aeschylus replies in a censorial spirit:

> Poets should hide a deed of shame, not introduce it or
> produce it.

Then he adds the essence of didacticism and utilitarianism:

> The little boys have schoolmasters to tell them what's
> the right thing.
> But adults have the poets. So then, certainly and surely,
> We must say things that are good for all . . .

It is hard to say here whether Aristophanes himself seriously believed in this moralistic and didactic view of poetry, for we must not fall into the fallacy of assuming that a character in a play voices its author's own opinion. Aristophanes' primary aim was to make people laugh, and it may be that many members of the audience hooted with laughter at the absurdity of this view. But on the other hand since the doctrine is agreed by both contestants, and is not disputed by Dionysos, it may have been the prevalent view of Athenians at the end of the fifth century. (In times of war utilitarianism flourishes.)

Yet in one sense at any rate this alleged poetic didacticism is palpably absurd. The idea that Homer provided a practical manual of military science for fifth-century Athenians as Aeschylus suggested cannot have been seriously credited. And Orpheus in early mythology seems to have been much more of a shamanistic singer with supernatural powers than a teacher and reformer, whatever the fifth-century Orphics may have claimed. (We know nothing for certain about Mousaios, if he ever existed.) To confuse the Homeric kind of poet with the Hesiodic is quite illegitimate, as Hesiod himself warned in his *Theogony*.

However it well suited Plato's purpose as a detractor of poetry to expose and satirize these extravagant claims – claims, it must be emphasized, not made by Homer himself. In the *Ion* a rhapsodist – typical or caricatured? – who holds them is easily refuted and humiliated by Socrates. In the *Republic* Homer is specifically blamed for his inadequacy as a teacher of useful information. It is as if the Founder of Christianity were to be blamed for the absurd pretensions of his medieval followers to pontificate about matters of science.

On the other hand, as is so often the case with Plato, in the *Phaidros* and the *Laws*[8] Socrates-Plato shows a much more sympathetic attitude to poets and towards Homer in particular. (Who can grasp and hold this Proteus?) He conceded that the poetic art could be divinely inspired and at times could grasp the truth with the aid of the Graces and Muses. He even adopted a factualistic attitude in one phrase, where he allowed that the poets with the help of the Graces and Muses can 'comprehend many events that really happened'. But it is the doctrine of the *Republic* – poets as faulty teachers – that has prevailed in modern criticism.

Aristotle in his *Poetics* had nothing to say about the didactic functions of poetry, presumably because he considered them incidental to its nature and purpose. In fact his assertion that a poet is entitled to alter facts to suit his art implicitly rejects the notion that poets should be teachers. For him *mimesis* is the essential quality of poetry. That is why he refuses to grant the title of poet to a teacher and scientist writing in metre like Empedocles. On the question whether bad characters in poetry do harm by setting a bad example he states that characters in tragedy should be *chrestá*, a vague term which probably here means little more than 'decent', 'respectable', rather than 'virtuous'.[9] When he goes on to say that in one play the character of Menelaos was 'unnecessarily' base, the implication is that tragedy is entitled to portray bad characters provided that they are not out-and-out melodramatic villains. In a later passage, which will be quoted in my section on the 'character-as-author' fallacy, Aristotle emphasizes that statements and deeds in literature should be judged in terms of the character involved and his motives not in terms of ideal morality as Plato so palpably did. In other words, if you want to make moral judgments about characters in fiction, for Heaven's sake be intelligent about it and don't try to impose inflexible rules.

One of the most striking features of the *Poetics* is Aristotle's emphasis on the importance of the pleasure-giving elements in poetry and art. He refers to them, in one way or another, twelve times – the pleasure of a happy ending (a vulgar one, he says), the pleasure of experiencing pity and fear in poetic form (which he implies is the special pleasure of poetry), the pleasure to be derived from a well-structured unity, the pleasures of the musical, rhythmical and visual elements, the pleasure of 'the marvellous' (proved by the fact that 'everyone exaggerates when telling things, because it gratifies people'), the pleasure of hearing an action presented in a condensed fashion (in comparison with the greater amplification of epic poetry), and the pleasure which is supreme for philosophers and laity alike, as Aristotle rather optimistically believes – that is, the pleasure of learning and making inferences, as when we recognize someone in a portrait. (This last in subtler forms is certainly one of the greatest pleasures of scholarship – for an archaeologist when he recognizes that a Mycenaean helmet can be identified with a helmet described in *Iliad* X, for a textual critic when he realizes that a puzzling jumble of letters can be identified with an intelligible key-word, for a literary critic when he sees the relevance of an enigmatical phrase. It is the same with all discoveries and recognitions in science and art. But sometimes, as we have seen in earlier chapters, the apparent illumination is a will-o'-the-wisp, and the epiphany is a mirage.)

It may be well to expand a little here on this hedonistic doctrine of poetry, because there is often a strong reluctance among critics to accept its primary importance. As we have seen in an earlier chapter, Homer, in contrast with Hesiod, implied that to give pleasure is the chief aim of poetry. He made Odysseus express this view very emphatically in his after-dinner speech among the Phaeacians in *Odyssey* IX. There Odysseus asserts that there is no achievement more delightful (*télos chariésteron*) than when gladness of heart (*euphrosúne*) prevails among banqueters enjoying ample food and wine and bardic song. 'Indeed', he adds, 'this to my mind seems to be a most beautiful (or 'most noble', or 'very fine', *kálliston*) feeling in our hearts'. Later moralists, including Plato in the *Republic*, considered this a reprehensible piece of hedonism. 'Does this seem to you to foster self-control when a youth hears it?' Plato asks.[10] (One ancient commentator tried to modify the hedonism by altering part of a line so as to say 'provided that baseness is absent', ignorantly using a non-Homeric form in this 'improvement'.)

Attitudes towards pleasure in general and towards the particular pleasure of poetry had varied widely among the pre-Socratic philosophers. The earliest recorded dictum on the subject is horrifyingly bleak. Pythagoras is alleged to have said: 'Sufferings are a good thing, but pleasures are in every way a bad thing: we came here for punishment and we ought to be punished.' In contrast, Democritos, 'the laughing philosopher', whose *summum bonum* was contentment (*euthumía*), made pleasure the pivot of his ethics, while emphasizing that 'Moderation (*sophrosúne*) increases delights and makes pleasures greater'. Antisthenes, the proto-cynic, accepted no pleasure except that of hard work and warned his followers to avoid studying literature. Plato's attitude in his *Republic* stands closer to Pythagoras' penitential creed than to Democritos'.[11]

Aristotle, with his emphasis on pleasure and especially on the deep psychological pleasure of tragic poetry, offered the strongest refutation of the anti-hedonistic doctrine. He was not an out-and-out hedonist as Epicurus was. But, like Democritos, he fully and freely recognized the pleasure principle as a salient motive in human contact. In his *Nicomachean Ethics*[12] he emphasized the supreme importance of teaching children to feel pleasure and pain at the right kinds of things, citing Plato in support of this. There the pleasure principle is seen to be as important for education as it is seen to be for poetry in the *Poetics*.

Thanks to Aristotle's defence and to the general Greek bias towards hedonism, most of the later literary critics rejected the puritanical approach to poetry and art. But among philosophers the Stoics with their insistence on stern duty were inclined to take a utilitarian view. Their rivals the Epicureans, who might have been expected to support literary hedonism, opposed literary and artistic pursuits in general as being harmful to their desired imperturbability. Epicurus himself dismissed the 'fool-fables' of Homer and described poets as a noisy rabble.[13] The later Epicurean Philodemos flatly rejected the view that the Homeric poems were didactic or moralistic, or that poets possessed special knowledge, or, indeed, that there was any significant relationship between poetry and reality, allegorical or otherwise. His general attitude was that since poetry played a large part in the life of his time he had to write about it, but that ultimately it was rather a useless phenomenon.

One milder contribution to the debate about the moral and educational value of poetry deserves more than a brief mention here. Plutarch in his essay 'How Youth should Study Poetry' meets some of the traditional objections with characteristic reasonableness. He contends that poetry is educationally valuable because it serves as a good introduction to philosophy, provided that youths are carefully cautioned about the kind of falsehoods that poets tell and about the emotional disturbances that poetry can cause. Poetry should not be banned or censored. Teachers should not treat their pupils as Ulysses treated his crew when his ship was approaching the island of the Sirens, when he prevented them from hearing the seductive Siren-song by blocking their ears with wax, while he himself, bound to the mast, heard it in safety. Instead of making their pupils deaf like that, teachers should ensure that all their pupils were safely bound to the mast of sound reason. Then they would sail safely onwards on their voyage of life, strengthened by the experience of having heard poetry's siren-song.

Plutarch goes on to argue that poetry is a mimetic art. (Here he quotes the fallacious aphorism of Simonides, 'Poetry is vocal painting, painting, silent poetry', which will be criticized on a later page.) Consequently, while one must not admire or imitate deeds that are ugly or evil, one can take pleasure in admiring the artist's or poet's skill in his imitation of them – good Aristotelian doctrine, this. Youths must be trained to recognize that evil words or evil deeds produced by evil characters in literature are not necessarily those of the poet. (This recalls Catullus's dictum that 'It is fitting for a dutiful [*pium*] poet to be chaste, but not necessarily his little verses.') Allegorical interpretations of immoral incidents in the Homeric poems and elsewhere are to be rejected, Plutarch believes. Further, readers of poetry must be careful not to admire heroes like Achilles too much – advice which might have saved some brilliant young English classicists from volunteering for the Dardanelles campaign in 1915.

Plutarch effectively exemplifies his principles with examples from Homer. He explains, for example, that it is wrong to blame Nausicaa for over-boldness and lack of restraint in her frank remarks in *Odyssey* VI about wanting to marry a man like Ulysses: it showed insight and prudence if she preferred him to 'some sailor or dancing man of her own townsmen'. Less elevated is a suggestion about Ulysses' sleepiness when the Phaeacians put him ashore on Ithaca: perhaps it was a ruse to avoid tipping them. All in all, poetry in Plutarch's view is useful for the insights it gives into human character and for its examples of virtue. So youths should study it, under careful direction, as a preparation for philosophy (just as the more tolerant among the Fathers of the Christian Church allowed the study of pagan poetry for a similar reason, as a *praeparatio evangelii*).

In that way Plutarch did his best to defend poetry from its more fanatical enemies. His whole essay is full of moderation and common sense. But in its total effect it must be regarded as hostile by all who maintain the Aristotelian charter of poetic autonomy.

Besides the philosophers, the scientists took sides in the quarrel between hedonists and utilitarians. Eratosthenes maintained that poets aimed at emotional effect (*psuchagogia*, literally 'leading the psyché') not teaching, and that one should not judge poems by their intellectual content or seek scientific and historical information in them. He quoted errors of fact in the Homeric poems to support this view. Against him Strabo the geographer argued that Homer was a useful and authentic source of information and quoted passages where Homer was scientifically accurate.[14] Horace in his *Ars Poetica*[15] offered a Roman compromise: to win general approval a poet should combine the useful and the enjoyable, the *utile* with the *dulce*. That great eighteenth-century critic in the Roman tradition, Samuel Johnson, said much the same: 'The end of writing is to instruct; the end of poetry is to instruct by pleasing.'[16]

The sterner Fathers of the early Christian Church preached a penitential and ascetic ethic close to the Pythagorean principle: 'we came here to be punished and we ought to be punished'. This remained the prevailing doctrine, in theory at least, until the end of the medieval period, though pleasurable poetry managed to survive it. The openly humanistic mood of the renaissance made literary and artistic hedonism respectable again. Shakespeare could confidently tell his audience that he wrote all for their delight. The subsequent era of puritanism gave way to Restoration gaiety and licentiousness, to be followed by the elegant hedonism of the Augustans. After it in a similar rotation came the renewed puritanism or neo-Jansenism of the early nineteenth century, then the rise of aestheticism, and then the neo-puritanism of Marxism and the joyless freedom of Freud.

Strangely enough even some of the strongest champions of

poetry in the more modern period have often been reluctant to emphasize the pleasure principle. Sidney, Shelley and Arnold preferred to defend poetry on didactic or moralistic or neoplatonic grounds. Wordsworth, however, in the preface to *Lyrical Ballads*, boldly asserted the primacy of what he called 'the grand elementary principle of pleasure', which constitutes 'the naked and native dignity of man', and by which man 'knows, and feels, and lives, and moves'. In a time when evangelical fervour, with its Pythagorean message of sin and sorrow in life's vale of tears, prevailed (though some Evangelicals managed to be jolly enough themselves), this last phrase of Wordsworth's must have sounded almost like a blasphemous parody of Saint Paul's words to the Athenians about the supreme deity 'in whom we live and move and have our being'. Plainly Wordsworth did not mean to advocate grossly sensual pleasures in a Baudelairean way. Yet the earnestness of his biblical phrase shows how deeply he believed that pleasure was a high and honourable and essential motive in art.

The aestheticists and amoralists who emerged in literature and art after Wordsworth's time gave the pleasure-principle a bad reputation and confirmed puritanical suspicions that hedonism was the path to moral perdition, with Baudelaire and Oscar Wilde as its supreme exemplars. Later one might have expected that the rebels against conventional morality after the First World War would have favoured a return to a hedonistic theory of literature and art. But on the whole the intellectual leaders preferred to base their doctrines on concepts such as self-expression, or the life force, or the welfare state, rather than on pleasure pure and simple. Even amoralists, it seems, can be puritanical. Freud, who wrote so effectively about 'the pleasure principle', depreciated the pleasurable element in literature as escapism. Fiction, as he saw it, was an unworthy day-dream or anodyne, the opposite of 'reality' (that old Proteus-enemy of poetic truth).

This reluctance to accept pleasure as a primary motive in poetry and art lies very deep in contemporary classical criticism.

If a lecturer ventures to assert that poetry is primarily for pleasure, many of his hearers are likely to suspect that the lecturer is not a serious scholar but only a dilettante, an amateur. The fact that these two words, with their emphasis on enjoyment, are so often used pejoratively testifies to the general prejudice against scholastic hedonism.

Objections to insistence on the pleasure-principle in literary appreciation seem to me to be wrong for three main reasons. First, to present a hedonistic literature as if it were designed primarily for didactic or moralistic reasons is unfair to the authors and misleading for intending readers. Second, when pleasure is unquestionably a dominant motive in human life, is it educationally justifiable to minimize the sensuous and intellectual pleasure that poetry can give? Third, is it not a fact that Homer and other early poets survived much better than the prose-writers who criticized them so forcefully because of the delight that they gave to their hearers? Of course every mature teacher is aware of the dangers caused by undisciplined hedonism and by the excess so often preached against by the ancient Greeks. But bad as this can be for the individual and for society, has it done more social harm than puritanism and penitential morality?

We still have to consider what Plato regarded as the most serious moral objection to the poets, especially the dramatists. In the last book of the *Republic* Socrates finally condemns them because they excite the emotions excessively and overthrow the control of reason in the *psyché*. This is a disconcerting doctrine for those scholars and teachers who present Greek tragedy as essentially an intellectual experience. But in Greek theatrical history from the incident at Phrynichos' *Capture of Miletos* onwards there is evidence that audiences at the tragic performances could be very strongly moved.[17] Athenian drama with its music and dancing and rhythmical speech commanded emotive elements which modern drama has mainly lost. Besides, it was ultimately a Dionysiac liturgy, and it may well have been that something of the primal Dionysiac frenzy was revived in the audience when the performance was especially dynamic. At any rate there is no doubt that Plato saw dangerous emotionalism in the theatre of his time. So, for the sake of society as he desired it to be, he issued his decree of almost total banishment of the poets from his ideal State – censorship, the ultimate sanction against the poets' refusal to conform to non-poetic principles.

Plato recognized and advocated two kinds of censorship in the *Republic*. In the earlier part it seems that he would have been satisfied with the deletion of specific offending passages, but later he opted for total banishment. Curiously enough, he did not lay any emphasis on indecent or obscene language as a reason for condemnation. Presumably this was because the phallic element in the Dionysiac cult as presented in the theatrical festivals still had strong religious support when he was young. Aristotle, however, born after the great epoch of Old Comedy, asserted in his *Politics* that shameful speech (*aischrologia*) should be censored.[18] On this principle some of the Hellenistic commentators proceeded to tamper with the texts of the Greek poets. For example[19] in *Iliad* IX, where Phoenix states that to please his mother and to spite his father he had sexual intercourse with his father's concubine, editors inserted two negatives to make Phoenix refuse to do so – rather ignorant editors, it seems, as the alteration ruined the metre. Aristarchos, apparently believing that thoughts of parricide were worse than adultery, deleted the subsequent lines in which Phoenix says that he had thought of killing his father. (Plutarch reasonably explained these immoralities as salutary examples of what anger can cause.)

In modern times censorship by alteration or deletion reached its heyday when the notorious Dr Bowdler (a medical man, not a clergyman) produced his 'family editions' of Shakespeare and Gibbon. One at least of his followers exceeded him in zeal. The Reverend Charles William Stocker produced an edition of Herodotos in 1831, in which he thought fit to reduce the whole of the second book to a single page in his determination 'to expunge every expression which was in the least objectionable'.[20] Some degree of bowdlerization remained the rule in school editions of the classics by English-speaking scholars until well into the twentieth century. Regardless of poetic unity they suppressed passages from the text, often with little or no indication of their deletion. Now, however, when literature in plain English has become so outspoken, few editors feel the need for censorship. Yet it can still occur: a recent edition of Catullus omitted almost one-third of the poems because they do not 'lend themselves to comment in English'. Why choose to edit a poet at all on those terms?

The second kind of censorship, total banning, has also had a long history from Cleisthenes of Sicyon through the *Index Expurgatorius* to modern censorship boards. The English puritans were as energetic as the Roman Curia in this. But it was also an English puritan who voiced the strongest plea for literary freedom before Voltaire – John Milton in his *Areopagitica* in 1644. As a poet he believed in the sacred power of the Logos.

Yet, despite the poets' natural desire for freedom of speech can defenders of poetry who are also concerned with the well-being of society unreservedly condemn Plato's passionate warnings against the demoralizing effects of literature? Can we in the present climate of violence in our civilization totally reject his view that some kinds of literature – even of the higher sort – may make us worse people and worse citizens by causing us to imitate acts of immorality or by exciting our passions? Are we not all bound by the maxim, *Salus populi suprema lex*? To take a notorious modern case: were the atrocious Moors murders in England some years ago, with their appalling mutilations of child victims, the result of the murderers having read the works of Sade and of similar authors whose books were found in their possession?[21] Or had they read those books because they were already inclined to such atrocities? Again, when a youth in Scotland asserted that he had caused a huge fire as a result of seeing an incendiary film called *The Towering Inferno*, was he stating a fact or had he been a pyromaniac before seeing the film?

Unfortunately no clear verdict on cause and effect has been

established by psychologists or penologists on this far-reaching problem. Psychologists on the whole seem to accept some version of Aristotle's theory of catharsis and say that scenes of violence, cruelty and terror in literature and art may do more good than harm. On the other hand, officials responsible for law and order, and also many teachers, believe that Plato was right. If the second view is the true one, if it could be clearly proved, or even shown to be highly probable, that productions of *King Oedipus* encourage murder, incest, suicide and self-mutilation, or that the reading of Sade will cause further atrocities against children, what decent person could refuse to sanction some degree of censorship? On the other hand there are so many possible causes of cruelty and violence in the world that it must seem unjust to single out literature and art for the strictest control – and even more unjust to single out, as Plato did, poetry as the chief offender. Plato presumably launched his main attack on the poets because of their special skill in exploiting the seductive power of the spoken word. No medium of communication in his day, not even oratory, could affect people so strongly as poetry. But that argument does not hold now.

In the end the defence of poetry against Plato's theory of demoralizing mimesis rests on the validity of some kind of catharsis. I shall cite only one rather neglected kind of testimony in its favour. It is taken from the writings of two modern poets whose personal feelings are well known, Tennyson and Arnold. Tennyson in his younger period as a poet felt intensely the agonies of what is now called 'the search for identity'. Like many another Victorian, he sensed in himself conflicting forces of purity and lust, energy and lethargy, asceticism and self-indulgence, elation and despondency, hope and despair. By letting his imagination blend with what was known of historic hero-figures he found a catharsis for himself. In his poem on the stylite hermit, Saint Simeon, he embodied the antinomies of saint and sinner; in the 'Lotos-Eaters' and in 'Ulysses' he set listless lethargy against heroic endeavour; in 'Sir Galahad' he apotheosized purity; in 'Tithonus' he explored his constant preoccupation with physical decline and death; and in the Sir Lancelot of the *Idylls of the King* he entered into the spirit of a man torn between faith and faithlessness, honour and dishonour. Tennyson said himself that after the death of his friend Arthur Hallam, the writing of his poem on Ulysses had helped him in 'going forward and braving the struggle of life perhaps more simply than anything in *In Memoriam*'.[22]

One could easily trace the same cathartic effect in other poets of the romantic period who found self-confidence through a sense of shared identity with heroic or tragic figures from the past – and all in a time before psycho-analysis had tried to illuminate what Dante called the dark lake of the heart. If we knew more about the lives of the Greek and Roman epic and dramatic master-poets of the past we might have evidence that they, too, were finding themselves in some of their chief characters – Aeschylus, accused of impiety, in Prometheus; Sophocles, perhaps after a personal failure, in Ajax; Euripides, perhaps distressed by eroticism in his time, in Hippolytos. But in the absence of evidence for the personal feelings of the classical poets such speculations are baseless.

What happened to Tennyson, if what I have suggested is right, was the beneficial result of the kind of mimesis which Plato thought harmful in his *Republic*, the kind which involves such a high degree of empathy that one's own character and personality are merged for a while in the subject of a poem. This process of imaginative self-identification with another person is different from the kind of mimesis that consists in choosing some saint or hero for purposeful imitation in one's life, as in a Christian's use of *The Imitation of Christ* by Thomas à Kempis. There we have a conscious and deliberate act of the will, while Tennyson's kind of catharsis by mimesis may have been largely unconscious – he thought he was writing a poem about Ulysses and found in the end that he had written a poem about his own psychological state.

One may find the same contrast between conscious and unconscious mimesis in poems by Matthew Arnold. When he began a sonnet with the question

> Who prop, thou ask'st, in these bad days, my mind?

and went on to say that his props were Homer, Epictetos and especially Sophocles, he was writing with cool intellectual detachment and there was no suggestion of personal empathy. But it is otherwise in his *Scholar-Gipsy*, based on Glanvil's story of 'a lad in Oxford' who left his studies and joined the gipsies and came to believe that 'they had a traditional kind of learning among them, and could do wonders by the power of imagination, their fancy binding that of others . . .' Here Arnold implicitly contrasts the melancholy sadness of his own heart with the spirit of the Scholar-Gipsy 'free from the sick fatigue, the languid doubt' and exempt from 'this strange disease of modern life, With its sick hurry, its divided aims, Its heads o'ertax'd, its palsied hearts'. He admires this liberated academic for his unfailing idealism

> Still nursing the unconquerable hope,
> Still clutching the inviolable shade

in contrast with those of Arnold's own circle

> Who fluctuate idly without term or scope,
> Of whom each strives, nor knows for what he strives,
> And each half lives a hundred different lives;
> Who wait like thee, but not, like thee, in hope.

Yet despite the profound sadness of this contrast between the responsible citizen and the escapist vagrant, Arnold finds images of new adventure and fortitude in the vivid concluding simile of his poem. He leaps in imagination away from Oxford and Victorian England to an island in the Aegean in the earliest days of Greek enterprise. He sees a 'merry Grecian coaster come', bringing

> The young light-hearted Masters of the waves,

and sees, too, 'the grave Tyrian trader' stealthily watching their arrival – as Arnold in imagination had watched the Scholar-Gipsy. But now the catharsis is achieved. The Tyrian trader – Arnold's surrogate – did not just sit down and groan about his ill fortune. On the contrary, like Ulysses at the end of Tennyson's poem, he

> snatch'd his rudder and shook out more sail,
> And day and night held on indignantly
> O'er the blue Midland waters with the gale,
> Betwixt the Syrtes and soft Sicily
> To where the Atlantic raves . . .

The despondency and apathy have gone: a new world of enterprise lies ahead.

What these poets themselves felt empathetically in composing such poems countless readers have felt in reading them and in reading all the masterpieces of literature from the *Iliad* to *Waiting for Godot*. Yet – to return to the main theme of this chapter – these imaginative creations were certainly not composed for didactic or moralistic or utilitarian purposes. They were composed because it was in the nature of their composers to produce them in response to life and art. In the same way Homer and his successors were artists not preachers, explorers not do-gooders. But by one of life's ironies while so many innumerable sermons and ethical treatises fall into oblivion in every century, these explorations of the human spirit never lose their power to make life more enjoyable and more endurable.

Chapter Six

Twenty-six Fallacies of Classical Criticism

Several fallacies have already been noticed in the previous chapters. Many of them stem from the basic fallacy of factualism. In the following pages others are added. Some go back to the earliest period of European literary criticism. Others are comparatively recent in identification if not in origin. One of them, *paralogismós*, is regularly exploited by creative writers in order to win credence from their audiences. Probably further types could be added, but these seem to me to be the commonest in classical editions and interpretations, including my own.

PARALOGISMÓS, THE FALLACY OF FALSE INFERENCE

This fallacy works in two ways – as an essential element in the art of poetry and as a deep source of misunderstanding among critics of poetry. (It is also, as Aristotle notices in his *Sophistical Refutations*, a method of argument frequently used by orators.) In the *Poetics* Aristotle mentions it in connection with that statement of his which is so congenial to defenders of poetry – 'Homer especially has taught the others to tell falsehoods in the right way'. This, he explains, is done by the use of *paralogismós*.[1] It works like this: if a certain proposition (call it *A*) is untrue but you want people to believe it, then if there is another proposition (call it *B*) which regularly follows as a consequence of *A*, add *B* to your statement; then people, knowing that B is true will tend to conclude that A must also be true. He exemplifies this process from the scene in *Odyssey* XIX, where Penelope first encounters Odysseus in disguise. Odysseus in order to persuade Penelope to believe a fictitious story about his having seen Odysseus in Crete describes details of his dress which she knows to be true. She falls into *paralogismós* by reasoning like this: 'If the stranger's story were true, he would be able to describe what Odysseus wore: he can describe what Odysseus wore, therefore his story is true.'

In the same way, Aristotle says, readers of poetry are deceived by the *paralogismoí* of the poets: because we know that a consequent fact is true, our *psyché* makes the erroneous inference that an antecedent statement is a fact. The admixture of truth gives verisimilitude to the falsehood.

I have not translated the word *psyché* in the last quotation because it carries a nuance, I believe, which has been generally overlooked. Scholars have often translated it as 'mind' here, making the process an entirely intellectual one. But *psyché* implies the whole sentient, emotional and intellectual self, not simply the rational element. Penelope *wants* to believe that the stranger has seen her husband, and this desire weakens her logic. It is the same with sympathetic readers of poetry: they *want* to believe its 'falsehoods'. Here Aristotle, I believe, is hinting at the notion expressed by Coleridge in his celebrated phrase, 'a willing suspension of disbelief'.

Something similar to this frequently happens to historicistic critics, as we have seen in an earlier chapter. They want to believe that Homer is describing Troy VIIA or the Mycenaean palace at Ano Englianos. They can point to a few details in which Homer's descriptions do in fact correspond closely with Mycenaean artefacts. Then, like Penelope, they believe that because some details are trustworthy the rest of the story is trustworthy.

Shortly after his discussion of *paralogismós* in the *Poetics* Aristotle goes on to illustrate another method of gaining credence for improbable fictions. He does not actually call it by the same name, but it is obviously very similar to *paralogismós*.

He has just been dwelling on the theme that a poet should avoid impossibilities or improbabilities as far as possible. If these are unavoidable the poet should use all his skill to make them imperceptible by 'sweetening' them with his poetic art. He cites the passage in *Odyssey* XIII where Odysseus sleeps undisturbed while the Phaeacians transfer him and his possessions from their ship to the shore of Ithaca. In the hands of an inferior poet the incident would be quite incredible. So much bustle and activity would be bound to awaken even the deepest sleeper. Homer exerts his highest skill to make the incident plausible. He first distracts our attention from the sleeping hero by vividly comparing the speeding ship with a four-horsed chariot in full course and with a swooping hawk. Then he produces his famous description of the Harbour of Phorcys and the Cave of the Nymphs. With these similes and descriptions still vivid in our minds while Odysseus is being put ashore, we never think of asking why Odysseus failed to waken when the Phaeacians were moving him from their ship. We are so happy and contented in the poet's entrancing world that our critical faculties stay as sound asleep as Odysseus while we let the story carry us on. Nor does Homer's skill relax after the deed is done. He makes sure that we shall not have any critical afterthoughts. Immediately after Odysseus has been set ashore the scene is changed to Olympos with Poseidon storming up to Zeus to demand punishment for the Phaeacians. We have no time to look back if we want to stay with the action. This is like the conjuror's art of distracting our attention from what he is doing with one hand by doing something spectacular with the other. We are so well satisfied with what the distracting gestures provide that we do not repudiate the results achieved by the other hand.

A passage from a post-Aristotelian poet illustrates the paralogistic element in this kind of writing even more clearly than the Ithacan episode. Theocritos in his Hylas idyll skilfully gives an appearance of reality to the quite impossible climax of the poem. First he presents a botanically plausible list of plants growing round a pond in the forest – rushes, celandine, maidenhair fern, wild celery and dog's-tooth grass. Then he introduces the water-nymphs, giving them enchantingly euphonious names, Eunika and Malis and Nucheia 'with spring-time in her eyes'. Then come the impossibilities, scientifically speaking. The nymphs drag Hylas down into the pond and try to comfort him. He, under the water, hears his friend Heracles calling for him in the forest. Hylas calls back, but his voice, muted by the water, sounds to Heracles as if it came from far away, and Heracles fails to find him. The idea that a boy could call from under water is, of course, physically absurd. But the *paralogismós* of the botanical descrip-tion and the incantation of the lovely names make it easy to accept.

All great fiction-writers employ varieties of *paralogismós* to give verisimilitude to their stories, drawing us into a world that is both non-factual and credible, a world of 'make-believe'. In a sense, then, they are partly themselves to blame when factual-ists are deluded into believing them literally. The poets use their delusive arts to enable their audiences to live for a while in a dream world, but they expect them, when the poem is done, to return consciously to the waking world. They find to their dismay that some of their audience cannot tell when the dream is over.

THE FALLACY OF IMPROPRIETY

As has been already exemplified, a recurrent criticism of poetry from as early as the sixth century of the pagan era was that poets said improper things about the gods and heroes. This kind of criticism was intensified in the Alexandrian era when the royal courts of the Macedonian monarchs in Alexandria and elsewhere had introduced oriental patterns of behaviour, perhaps partly modelled on the Persian style, making as great a difference from the *mores* of the previous democratic city-states as that between Tudor and Victorian England. Alexandrian editors of Homer deplored the fact that in *Odyssey* XIX the goddess Athena carried a lamp – even though it was a golden one – like a servant. They censured Nausicaa's frankness about matrimonial affairs in *Odyssey* VI as indecorous, and Odysseus' careful counting of his Phaeacian gifts in *Odyssey* XIII as parsimonious. Two words they used in their condemnations were *aprepés*, 'improper, unseemly', and *euteleís*, 'cheap'.

Such neglect of the principle *autres temps autres moeurs* recurs in various forms all through classical criticism. Leaf in his note on *Iliad* II, 791–5, approves of Aristarchos' obelization of the passage partly on the grounds that 'the message is not adapted to the tone of a son speaking to his father, but is intense and reproachful'. For 'a son' read 'an Alexandrian, or a Victorian son'. Or again, in the present climate of opinion one can only laugh sardonically when Leaf remarks on a Mycenaean seal depicting a bare-breasted woman – 'The drawing suggests that the body was naked above the waist, but that is hardly credible.'[2]

Prejudices of this nature can cause even the best of scholars to perform extraordinary exegetical contortions. Gladstone offers an amusing example in his generally very perceptive and enlightened *Studies on Homer and the Homeric Age* (1858). In *Odyssey* III, 464 ff., Homer plainly states that Polycaste, the youngest unmarried daughter of King Nestor, personally bathed Telemachos when he came on a visit to Pylos, and that she afterwards rubbed him with oil and dressed him in a tunic and cloak. Such lubricious behaviour among royal personages could hardly be condoned in the era of good Queen Victoria and of Albert the Good. Indeed, as Gladstone would know, earlier scholars, including the Archbishop of Thessalonica, Eustathios, had also been perturbed by it, though most of them had reluctantly accepted the incident as an example of 'primitive' manners. (One extension of the story removed the offensive implications: Telemachos married the girl later. Unfortunately Homer offered no ground for that happy solution.)

Gladstone faced the problem as resolutely as he faced political questions, and ultimately he believed that he had solved it. He candidly admitted that here and elsewhere in the Homeric poems princesses and demi-goddesses personally bathed adult males. But each description, he emphasized, should be examined very carefully for saving features. For instance in the description of how Circe bathed Odysseus Homer says only that Circe poured the water over his head and shoulders as he sat in the bath, which evidently implies that 'what may be called essential decency was observed'. (These nineteenth-century scholars, from Bowdler on, were remarkably perceptive, not to say imaginative, about scenes of that kind.) But, even with this reservation, what Circe could do without great impropriety hardly excused what Polycaste did according to the traditional interpretation. Circe was an experienced witch: Polycaste was an innocent young princess.

There were several possible expedients. The passage could be denounced as an interpolation. But there was only very weak support for that in the textual tradition. One could emend the crucial word (*loûsen*) which according to general usage meant 'she bathed him'. But Gladstone liked to preserve the reading of the manuscripts if possible. One could argue that Telemachos must have worn at least a minimum of decent covering during the process. But there was no reference to anything of the kind anywhere in Homer. Gladstone, a man of many devices like the wily Ulysses (as his political opponents openly proclaimed), chose a subtler explanation already suggested in the ancient scholia: the verb *loûsen* was causative not transitive: Polycaste caused Telemachos to be bathed. As Gilbert Wakefield had explained in his edition of Pope's *Odyssey*, 'the lady supplied Telemachus with the apparatus' (for bathing, lubrication and dressing) 'without personal application of them'. In other words the verb did not mean 'the performance of a particular operation', but 'the giving to the person concerned the means of doing it for himself'. The clever thing about this interpretation is that it is grammatically possible, as the most authoritative British editors of the *Odyssey*, Merry and Riddell, admitted. But they, after a masterly survey of the other references to women bathing men, show that Gladstone's interpretation is against Homeric usage. As a concession, however, to the prevailing morality of their time they emphasized that 'the scantiness of light in Homeric rooms was itself a veil – a consideration applicable to all the cases of indoor bathing, whatever we take the woman's part to have been.'

A glance at earlier comments may put Gladstone's view on Homeric propriety in better perspective. Alexander Pope in his translation of the *Odyssey* did not flinch from allowing Polycaste to bathe and anoint Telemachos. But the footnote on the passage shows some uneasiness:

> It is very necessary to say something about this practice of women bathing and anointing men; it frequently occurs thro' the whole *Odyssey*, and is so contrary to the usage of the moderns as to give offence to modesty; neither is this done by women of inferior quality, but we have here a young Princess, bathing, anointing, and cloathing the naked *Telemachus*. *Eustathius* indeed tells us, it was undoubtedly by her father's command [in fact Homer says nothing about that]: but if it was a piece of immodesty, it does not solve the objection, whoever commanded it. I confess it would be immodest in these ages of the world, and the only excuse that occurs to me is, to say that Custom establish'd it. It is in manners, in some degree, as in dress; if a fashion never so indecent prevails, yet no person is ridiculous, because it is fashionable; so in manners, if a practice prevails universally, tho' not reconcilable to real modesty, yet no person can be said to be immodest who comes into it, because it is agreeable to the custom of the times and countries.

One cannot be sure how much of this note was written by Pope himself and how much by his collaborators William Broome and Elijah Fenton. To my mind it looks as if the first part down to 'her father's command' was written by one or both of his helpers and the more tolerant remainder by Pope himself. At any rate the note as a whole recognizes the principle of *autres temps*, even if one deplores the tone of self-righteousness in 'tho' not reconcilable to real modesty' in Pope's era of over-dressed immorality.

If we go back a century or so to Chapman's translation we find no squeamishness about the incident:

> . . . Polycaste (call'd the fair,
> Nestor's young'st daughter) bathed Ulysses' heir;
> Whom having cleansed, and with rich balms bespread,
> She cast a white shirt quickly o'er his head . . .

This has the freshness and innocence of the Homeric scene. As Athenaeus[3] expressed it – and why did so few editors quote him? – 'Homer represents maidens bathing their guests, implying that they would not physically arouse men who had lived honourably and temperately'. In other words *Honi soit qui mal y pense*.

It is not always easy in matters of this kind to distinguish morals from manners, but every honest critic must try. With authors such as Martial, Rabelais, and Swift, their manners are often filthy, in so far as they describe disgusting actions and incidents, but their morals are, as they claim, good. No one has convincingly denied that Homer's morals are in general good, with occasional 'lapses' like the seduction of Zeus and the adultery of Aphrodite and Ares, or that his manners are generally admirable. Unlike Aristophanes, Homer never aims at shocking his audience, except about the horrors of war and violence. (Witness a phrase like 'his guts gushed out on the ground', *khúnto khamaì kholádes*, harsh in meaning and harsh in sound.) There is not the slightest hint of sexual prurience in his bath-scenes. They are presented as a pleasing convention of aristocratic society. The nudity in them was accepted as readily as was nudity among Victorian males when swimming together at Parson's Pleasure in Gladstone's Oxford and elsewhere – just as the bathing of male guests by women was normal in Scandinavia, Russia and Japan when Gladstone and the others were writing their commentaries.

Each epoch, of course, has its own standards of propriety and impropriety. At present we are more inclined to censure authors for elitism or racialism or class prejudice or imperialism or militarism than for sexual immorality or for vulgarity. The best scholars and critics will not be swayed by these. But when even such good scholars as Leaf and Murray (as will be illustrated on 'the egoistic fallacy') could be influenced by contemporary prejudices in the past, it is unlikely that the principle of *autres temps* – and indeed *autres pays* – will always be scrupulously observed in the future.

THE COSMETIC FALLACY: POETIC STYLE AS FANCY DRESS

This fallacy consists in believing that poetical language is a process of ornamentation, as when a writer on Greek mythology, as quoted in my first chapter, remarked that Spenser in his presentation of Una and the Red Cross Knight was 'merely putting into poetical form what he could have expressed in prose . . . and adorning it with the flowers of his inexhaustible fancy'. There is strong support for this view in antiquity. It is implied by Parmenides and Gorgias. Plato assumed it in some of his attacks on poetry, though it conflicts with the doctrine of poetic 'madness'. Aristotle also seems to have accepted it, to judge from his description of the stylistic qualities of poetic diction as 'flavourings' (*hedúsmata*) in the *Poetics*.[4] Lucretius regarded his poetical language as sweetening for his philosophic doctrine like honey on a bitter pill. Similarly Strabo[5] believed that Homer 'adorned' (*ekósmese*) his theme of the Trojan War with 'myth-makings'. But no classical poet, apart from those with an avowedly didactic purpose, expressed such a view.

Modern critics and poets have emphatically denied the cosmetic fallacy. In their opinion one cannot separate thought and expression in poetic composition: the relationship between them is more like that between body and soul than between a body and its dress. 'If words be not an incarnation of the thought, but only a clothing for it', Wordsworth observes in his essay 'Upon Epitaphs', 'then surely they will prove an ill gift . . .' Similarly Carlyle remarks in his *Sartor Resartus*, 'Language is called the Garment of Thought: however, it should rather be, Language is the Flesh-Garment, the Body of Thought'.[6] And, to quote a contemporary critic, 'ever since the romantic period metaphoric formulations employing the living integrity of thought and expression, matter and manner, content and form have been commonplaces of literary criticism'.[7] We remember, too, that A. E. Housman in his essay on the name and nature of poetry describes how 'a line or two of verse, sometimes a whole stanza' would flow into his mind at moments of inspiration. To the same effect Louis MacNeice recorded: 'I watched the words come and drink at my mind'.[8] There is no support here for the belief that the ideas and thoughts come first and then the poet dresses them in suitable poetic dress. On the contrary the words often come first and the 'meaning' afterwards: then the words choose the poets rather than the poets choose the words.

That refers to the initial stages in poetic composition, the inspirational phase. Afterwards, of course, comes the often slow and laborious process of 'polishing', the 'labour of the file' as Horace calls it in a metaphor from sculpture, the *ars* which perfects the products of the poet's *ingenium*. A great poet excels in both. Virgil, according to Donatus' *Life*, said that when he was composing his *Georgics* he used to dictate a large number of lines in the morning and spend the rest of the day licking them into shape as a she-bear was reputed to shape her cubs. (The simile implies that the matutinal verses were born, not made.) Plato, according to Dionysios of Halicarnassos, took great trouble with the opening sentence of his *Republic*.[9] James Joyce worked for a whole day on two sentences of his *Ulysses*.[10] Here the analogy from cosmetics is valid. The author is consciously and deliberately remodelling or ornamenting the first text of his projected work, as a woman 'makes up' her face. Paul Valéry emphasized the importance of this process:[11]

> [the poet] is no longer the disheveled madman who writes a whole poem in the course of one feverish night; he is a cool scientist, almost an algebraist, in the service of a subtle dreamer . . . He will take care not to hurl on to

paper everything whispered to him in fortunate moments
by the Muse of Free Association. On the contrary everything he has imagined, felt, dreamed and planned will
be passed through a sieve, weighed, filtered, subjected
to *form* . . .

Yet despite Valéry's insistence on the intellectual process in
the making of poetry, the poet is basically for him 'a subtle
dreamer'.

Because this second process of polishing the data of inspiration
is rational and systematic classical critics, ancient and modern,
have generally devoted almost all their attention to it rather
than to the inspirational phase – and rightly so since the latter
involves unsolved problems of the workings of the unconscious
mind. But they must resist the temptation to depreciate the
importance of the inspirational phase without which all the
cosmetic art in the world will fail to produce authentic poetry.
One can say *poema nascitur non fit* as truly as *poeta nascitur non fit.*

THE FALLACY OF POETRY-AS-PAINTING

If Plutarch is right in attributing to Simonides, who died in
468 BC, the dictum that poetry is 'speaking painting', and
painting, 'silent poetry',[12] then it is one of the oldest fallacies
in the European tradition. Many subsequent critics and
rhetoricians accepted Simonides' aphorism, notably the author
of the *Dissoi Logoi* and Isocrates, Plato, Cicero and the pseudo-
Longinus. (But Pindar repudiated a similar analogy between
poetry and sculpture – 'I am no statue-maker to produce
images standing idle on their base'.[13]) It was raised to a major
critical doctrine at the renaissance. From that time on it
was generally exploited in favour of painting rather than
poetry until Gotthold Lessing published his epoch-making
essay, *Laocoon: or On the Limits of Painting and Poetry*, in 1766.
Since then the analogy has generally been presented with
more careful reservations. But it is sometimes cited still in a
misleading way by literary critics, especially by those interested
in visual, rather than in audial, aspects of poetry.

The fallacy of the comparison lies in its half-truth. Obviously poets ancient and modern have presented scenes of people, places and things, which painters also presented. Also, as Lessing observed in his opening paragraph, both poets and painters 'represent absent things as if they were present, appearances as if they were realities; they both deceive, and the illusion is in both cases a pleasing one'. Further, Lessing adds, the source of the pleasure that both achieve is beauty, and in this process each can help the other with explanations and illustrations. In the rest of his essay Lessing concerns himself mainly with the nature of classical art, not poetry. But he makes one essential distinction: unlike the poet, 'the artist can never seize from ever-changing nature more than one single moment' and 'the painter, in particular, can only make use of this moment from one point of view'. (One could take exception to this in terms of large-scale painting in which the eye can travel from scene to scene as in a strip cartoon.) Also, painting can suggest movement and change by various methods. But in general it is true that painting (like sculpture) is momentary and poetry continuous. One can grasp the basic 'message' of a painting with one gaze (though its implications may be endless). To do the same with the *Iliad* would take something like seventeen hours, reading at the rate of fifteen lines a minute.

In other words, to enjoy a poem (and music) one has to submit to an extended process in time, while a painting can be perceived and enjoyed almost instantaneously. In that way poetry is kinetic, painting static. The essence of the poetic process is time (and the elements of its rhythms in classical poetry are mainly distinguished in terms of time), while the essence of painting is space. For those reasons a better analogy for poetry would be mimetic dancing – 'Poetry is a dance of words and ideas: dancing is a poetry of bodies and gestures.'

Further, there is a radical difference between visual images presented to the eye by visual lines, shapes and colours, and the mental images stimulated in the brain by words and sounds. The painter's pictures are prefabricated for the viewer.

The hearer or reader of poetry makes his own visualizations of what the words are intended to suggest: he provides his own illustrations, so to speak. It is true that paintings can be seen by different people in different ways according to their sensory and intellectual abilities. But a clear visual model is provided for all alike, while if each of us was asked to draw a picture of Achilles slaying Hector there would be endless differences – and while we might agree on what was improbable in any particular representation there would be no precise basis for agreeing on which of them was closest to Homer's visualization of the scene. This is one of the chief objections to illustrated works of fiction. The illustrations impose stereotyped images on the reader and inhibit their imaginations, just as elaborate scenery and other stage effects can inhibit a theatrical audience's imagination. Shakespeare and the Greek dramatists needed no aids of that kind to make their audiences feel that they were truly on the sea-coast of Bohemia or in Cloud-cuckoo-land.

There is one way in which poetry can, rather frivolously, get the direct visual effect of painting or drawing – by a pictorial use of writing. In Chinese, since the written symbols, being ideograms, often have some resemblance visually to their meanings, a poem can be a series of pictures as well as of ideas, and the brush-work of whoever writes the poem on paper can be as elegantly pictorial as any painting. Poets who use a non-pictorial alphabet cannot easily achieve that kind of effect. But European poets have occasionally exploited visual similarities between letters of the alphabet and natural phenomena. The Greek poet Aischrion described the crescent moon as 'the sky's fair letter C'. Dante saw a man's eyebrows, eyes and nose, in the medieval lettering of the Italian word for a man, OMO, and identified an inverted M with the head and neck of an eagle. The French poet Alfred de Musset described the sight of a full moon over a church spire as 'like the dot over an i'. Paul Maurice grandiloquently apostrophized Victor Hugo in the celebrated alexandrine:

Les tours de Notre Dame étaient l'H de ton nom.

(French poets are particularly subtle in these 'optical' effects, as I have exemplified elsewhere.[14]) The most emphatic example that I know of is e. e. cummings's

mOOn Over tOwn, mOOn.

There indeed poetry is speaking painting. But is it better poetry for that? The effect is amusing rather than inspiring – a kind of visual pun. Yet when a poet such as Dante uses it we can hardly call it trivial; and puns used to be regarded as being solemnly significant, as will be illustrated later.

Another example of a direct visual impact from poetry is to be found in the so-called shape-poems, in which the words are set out on the page in the shape of some object like an egg or an axe or an altar. These go back to the Hellenistic era. (Their popularity proves that by that time the oral tradition in Greek literature had been greatly weakened.) An extant poem in the shape of a shepherd's pipe is attributed to Theocritos, and an *Axe* and *Wings* to Simmias. Medieval writers produced some extraordinarily elaborate constructions of this kind. Renaissance poets also tried their hands at this hybrid art, and in England the popular writer on rhetoric George Puttenham gave detailed attention to it in his *Arte of English Poesie* in 1589. A delightful modern example is the Mouse's Tale (or Tail) in *Alice in Wonderland*, where the print curves and diminishes very mousetailistically. The Greeks called shape-poems 'technical pranks' (*technopaignia*), thereby distinguishing them from serious poetry.

A rather far-fetched notion may be mentioned here. One way of getting an exact analogy between poetry and painting would be by using an oscillograph to make a visual record of the sound-waves caused by reciting a poem. (Oscillograms are sometimes used, I believe, by police as a means of identifying persons suspected of crime: they speak certain words into the oscillograph and the resulting complex of lines has a unique shape for every speaker, because of the extraordinary individuality of every human voice.) One could then compare, say, the shape of a poem about Helicon or Popocatapetl with a photograph of the mountain or else with the mountain itself. Or one could compare oscillograms of the opening lines of the *Iliad* and of the *Odyssey* spoken by the same person. Conceivably – but barely so – a critical comparison of these two visualizations of the original sound-patterns might reveal factors undetectable acoustically, as an electrocardiograph can reveal cardiac conditions undetectable audially by a stethoscope.

While, then, the analogy between painting and poetry is on the whole misleading, yet there is much in common between the artistic aims of painters and poets. Both are concerned with formal patterns and with imaginative mimesis. And both, at the highest levels, seek to give pleasure rather than to record or instruct. When a viewer told Whistler that she had never seen a natural sunset like one of his paintings, he replied, 'But wouldn't you like to?'[15]

THE CHARACTER-AS-AUTHOR FALLACY

Aristotle in his *Poetics*,[16] probably in answer to Plato's strictures, warned moralistic critics against taking statements out of their context:

> As to whether something said or done in a poem is finely (*kalôs*) done or not, one should not merely consider whether the actual word or deed itself is worthy of respect or despicable, but one should also have regard to the doer or the sayer, the person he is dealing with, the time, the place, the means, and the motive – whether, for example, it was for the sake of achieving a greater good or to avoid causing a greater evil.

No competent scholar fails to observe this principle in its more obvious applications. When someone tells him about a statement in Psalm 114 that 'there is no God', he will check the context and find that the verse begins 'The fool has said in his heart . . .' Similarly when Saint Paul quoted Epimenides to the effect that all Cretans are liars,[17] the scholar will remember that Epimenides himself was a Cretan.

Yet when teachers, whether scholars or not, particularly admire some ethical statement in the works of an author whose name carries authority they may yield to a temptation to attribute statements made by a character to the author himself. One frequently finds Polonius' advice to his son in *Hamlet* quoted as if it gave us the considered opinion of Shakespeare:[18]

> This above all: to thine own self be true
> And it must follow as the night the day
> Thou canst not then be false to any man.

They forget that Polonius was a bumbling old hypocrite, and they ignore the fact that it would be as good a motto for a Casanova or a Hitler as for a Joan of Arc or Saint Francis – as presumably Shakespeare recognized. Because it supports vague notions of 'sincerity' and 'integrity' and, indeed, 'self-satisfaction', it is quoted as an authentic gem from the wisdom of the Supreme Bard. Its falsity is well shown up in *The Contest of Homer and Hesiod*. Hesiod asks Homer the riddle, 'What standard (*métron*) is most admirable and also most hateful for men?' Homer answers, 'To make oneself one's own standard is most admirable in the case of good men, but it is the worst of all things in the case of evil men.'

Aristophanes satirized this fallacy in his *Frogs*,[19] making Dionysos accuse Euripides of condoning perjury in his *Hippolytos* because its hero asserted the right to break an oath in certain circumstances. Euripides *may* in fact have believed in the universal validity of that right, but we may not presume that he did so from the words of a distinctly individualistic character in his play.

In questions of historicity, too, it follows that what a character says in fiction is even more suspect as regards factuality than what the author himself says. Sociologists have tried to extract sociological material from what characters say in Aristophanes and Dickens, disregarding the fact that exaggeration and distortion are staple qualities in the art of comedy. In the same way efforts have been made to deduce the prevailing attitude towards women in fifth-century Athens from remarks by characters in drama like Jason in the *Medea* or the chorus of Argive elders in the *Agamemnon*, against Aristotle's warning that the statements in poetry may be made only to suit the poet's artistic purposes. Aristotle does not fail to state as well that such statements *may* be factual, since facts are sometimes suitable for poetry. But, as we have seen, neither he nor anyone else has offered any means of separating the fact from the fiction on internal evidence.

A subtle extension of this fallacy has been well refuted in a recent book on Greek tragedy[20] – the assumption that 'the poet's teaching is contained in the words of certain of his lines, and so can be extracted from the work like a tooth'. This fallacy goes back at least as far as Aristophanes' comedies, though we cannot tell whether Aristotle himself believed it. Aristotle's remarks quoted at the beginning of this section are applicable here. Also we must recognize that 'admirable sentiments may be put in the mouth of a villain, and objectionable ones in the mouth of a virtuous character who does not act upon them (like Hippolytos's notorious "my tongue swore but my heart did not confirm it")'. Further, when a dramatist presents both sides of a case, as he should, which side are we to take as his own view?

Yet, despite these cautions, the desire to find an author's voice in his plays remains almost irresistible to many commentators, and of course their guesses may be right at times. At least they should always be qualified with 'perhaps' or 'possibly' – but not, I hope, with that egregious example of the egoistic fallacy 'I should like to think that . . .'

THE ETYMOLOGICAL FALLACY

In one serious study of Homer's *Odyssey*, as we saw in chapter Two, a scholar has argued that because there was a Greek word *penélops* meaning a duck, Penelope must have originally been a duck, 'the Penelops Kore of Arne'. In another serious study of folktale elements in the *Odyssey* the name of the grandfather of Odysseus, Arkeisios, is assumed to be derived from *árktos*, 'a she-bear', and an elaborate analogy between legends of Odysseus and folktales about the alleged 'Bearson' is based on this equation. Another reputable Homerist has suggested that there is evidence for trans-sexuality among the Homeric heroes in the fact that the name Patroclos when reversed is almost the same as Cleo-patra. Elsewhere the name Deianeira has been explained as 'Ought to Fall in Love Again', a linguistic improbability almost as absurd as some of the fantastic etymologies put forward in Plato's *Cratylos*.

One cannot positively disprove even the most far-fetched of these exegeses. But one can point to many examples in which what seems an obvious etymology is probably false (I give a more likely one in brackets): Jerusalem artichokes (probably from Italian *girasole*), rue des Echos in Laon (*rue des Escots*, named after the Irish scholars there in the Middle Ages), Gleneagles in Scotland (Gaelic *eaglais*, 'a church'). The Poodle Dog, a restaurant in San Francisco (said to have been originally Le Poulet d'Or, before the gold-miners became rich), Booterstown (from Irish *bothar*, 'a road'), Leopardstown ('lepers'), andirons (French *andier*), Kentish Town (Archbishop Cantaloupe), and the Court of Pie Powder (*pieds poudrés*).[21] I have heard a doctor when discoursing on man's mortality state that *homo* was etymologically connected with *humus*, and a beard-hater deriving 'barbarity' from *barba*, 'a beard'.

Such extravagances are mocked by Socrates in the *Cratylos* and parodied by Archbishop Whately in his amusing essay entitled 'Historic Doubts Relative to Napoleon Buonaparte' in which he offers a series of plausible etymologies to prove that Napoleon never existed. A similar essay by R. F. L. Littledale[22] purported to establish mainly by ingenious etymologies that Max Müller, the leading advocate of the solar interpretation of Greek myths, was himself a solar myth.

On the other hand while etymologies are often a fallacious

basis for theorizing about literature, they become valid material for literary criticism when they are used deliberately by authors. The belief that 'a name is an omen' (*nomen omen, ónoma órnis*) or 'a name has divine power' (*nomen numen*) pervades much of Greek literature from the earliest period. To give only three examples out of many: the name Odysseus is explained in the *Odyssey* as being derived from a verb meaning 'to incur wrath'; the Greek form of Ajax, *Aias*, is revealed as being a 'significant name' (*ónoma epónumon*) in Sophocles' play when in his agony of grief he groans *ai-ai*; when Pentheus is torn in pieces by frenzied maenads in the *Bacchai*, the doom decreed in his name (from *penthein* 'to suffer woe') becomes apparent. The ancient Greeks would have seen predestination in the name of the prelate who prompted, involuntarily it seems, public reference in England to the relationship between Edward VIII and Mrs Simpson – Bishop Blunt.

The ancient Greeks seem to have been particularly sensitive to etymological implications, as Plato's *Cratylos* so fully illustrates. Often their speculations were utterly absurd when viewed in the light of modern linguistics. But even the most absurd of them could suggest usable ideas and scenes to a poet's mind. Two strange and memorable passages in the *Odyssey* may exemplify this. In *Odyssey* XIX Penelope says that there are two Gates of Sleep, one of ivory through which false dreams emerge, the other of horn, through which true dreams come. (The image could symbolize poetic inspiration, but there is no hint of that in the context.) The word for ivory (*eléphas*) is close in form to the verb 'I deceive', *elephaíromi*. The word for 'horn' (*kéras*) is close to *kraíno*, 'I bring fulfilment'. Several scholars believe that the similarity of sound prompted the vivid image to the poet's mind.

Another possible example of etymological inspiration has not, I think, been identified before. It may be regarded as too far-fetched. But when one remembers the extraordinary elaborate and extended paronomasia with *oûtis* and *mêtis* which Homer employs in *Odyssey* IX, it may perhaps be acceptable. At the end of *Odyssey* XX an eerie and totally unpredictable scene occurs among the Suitors in the palace of Odysseus. One of them has just insolently thrown an ox's foot at Odysseus, still disguised as a beggar, and Telemachos has protested. One of the less violent Suitors then replies in a conciliatory way. His name is Agelaos, which, like other names such as Menelaos, Protesilaos and Archelaos, would normally suggest an etymological connection with *laós*, meaning 'people', or else possibly with *agéle*, 'a herd or group'. But what Spender calls the music of the word seems to have stimulated Homer's inner ear, for when Telemachos mentions Agelaos' name in his reply, he makes an anagrammatical pun between the vocative form *Agelae* and the Greek word for 'woes', *álgea*. This parono-masia is certainly not intended as a mere joke here, for the scene is tense and critical. Instead, the linguistic equation between *Agelae* and *álgea* symbolizes and embodies the direct connection between the Suitors and the woes of the house of Odysseus.

But Homer, if my surmise is correct, went further with this free linguistic association, with a very remarkable result. The name 'Agelaos' could also bear an etymological connexion with the negative prefix *a* – and the verb *gelân*, 'to laugh', so as to imply 'non-laughing' or 'laughing in an abnormal way', and this may have prompted the unexpected and unforgettable scene that follows. Given the situation that existed in Ithaca, we ourselves might have thought out the earlier quarrels between the Suitors and Odysseus – from 'probability', as Aristotle called it. But only a creative writer of genius could have produced this next episode.

Suddenly Athena intervenes. She arouses 'unquenchable laughter' among the Suitors and 'drives their wits astray'. First they laugh 'with alien jaws', and then they turn to weeping and lamentation, while an uncanny transformation of the whole scene takes place, and a prophet prophesies doom. Later the Suitors begin to laugh again in a normal, pleasant way, and the incident ends. It looks as if this strange by-play with the ideal of laughter, normal and abnormal, was inspired by a wild etymological connection rather than by a logical thought-process, for there is nothing in the preceding situation to suggest it. But here, as elsewhere, there can be no certainty about the workings of a poet's mind.

Down to Shakespeare's time in the English-speaking world etymological puns were still used for solemn effect, as in 'Old John of Gaunt and gaunt in being old'.[23] But in the eighteenth century literary fashion was turning against them, and punning gradually came to be regarded as something of a crime in sophisticated circles. At one Irish school in the 1920s there was a rule 'a pinch for a pun', with the merciful exception – 'Where no pun is meant there shall be no pun-ishment.' Puns returned to serious (or half-serious) literature in the later writings of James Joyce. *Finnegans Wake* is almost one long fugue of puns. Finally, it is a sobering thought that in Christian countries men and women have been burnt at the stake for disagreement about the meaning of a pun – 'Thou art Peter (*Pétros*) and on this rock (*pétra*) I shall build my church.'[24]

FALLACIES OF TIME

There are two main fallacies of this type. The first is hardly more than a relic from the past, the belief that in drama the time taken for the performance of events should correspond to the time that they would take in actuality. In the *Agamemnon* the interval between the announcement of the fall of Troy by the beacon-telegraph and the arrivals of the herald and Agamemnon is less than an hour, while the journey itself would have taken something like three days. Past commentators have thought it worth while to find some absurdity in this, but few would do so now. The earlier attitude was encouraged by insistence on the 'unity of time', falsely attributed as a rule of drama to Aristotle.

Ancient Greek audiences do not seem to have been perturbed by any such discrepancy. They did not confuse poetic time with natural time, knowing that in their own thoughts and in their dreams time could be telescoped or extended freely.

Psychologically that kind of time is more 'real' than time measured by the sun, moon or the stars.

A story told about a college don illustrates this. He dreamt that he was in London during the great plague, lying helpless and alone in an inner room. He heard a loud knock on his outer door. An age seemed to pass while he wondered whether the caller – perhaps one of those who used to shout 'Bring out your dead, bring out your dead' – would come in and help him. Eventually he heard another knock on his inner door. Then he awoke to find it was his servant coming to awaken him as usual. Less than a minute would have elapsed between the first knock and the second, but yet it seemed a long while to him. Another example: a man dreamt that someone was showing him large herds of cattle in a rich landscape, so he watched the scene with pleasure for a while. A metallic noise awoke him. It was the sound made by his servant as he put down the dreamer's morning kettle of hot water, having just said, 'Your kettle, sir', heard in his dream as 'Your cattle, sir' (which also illustrates how phonetic similarities can stimulate the imagination).

The other fallacy of time produced the not uncommon belief that 'anachronisms' are a fault in fiction. (The term is first found in a scholium on Aeschylus' *Prometheus* 845.) Well-known examples are the references to the Olympic Games in Sophocles' *Electra*, to Machiavelli in Shakespeare's *Henry VI*, to Aristotle in *Troilus and Cressida*, to a striking clock in *Julius Caesar*, to printing in *Henry IV*, billiards in *Antony and Cleopatra*, cannons in *King John*. Censure of this kind is another product of historicism. Time-shifts are as admissible in poetry as they are in our dreams. They are only to be censured when they harm the general poetic effect. The anachronistic clock that strikes the time in *Julius Caesar* gives a better dramatic effect than would have been given by an archaeologically appropriate waterclock. It does not matter whether these divagations from history are due to ignorance or not, provided that the illusion of actuality is preserved. Like Joshua in his battle against the Amorites or Zeus on his nuptial night with Alcmene, the poet

can make time stand still for his purposes, if he has the in-
cantatory power of high poetry to make his audience believe
him. Poetically there was good sense in the reply of an Irish
stationmaster to a criticism that the two clocks in his station
showed different times: 'What would be the good of having
two clocks if they showed the same time?'

It does not matter whether a poetic time-shift is due to
ignorance, carelessness or deliberate choice, so long as the
illusion of actuality is preserved – as Aristotle affirmed. When
Plato in his *Gorgias* conflated the death of Pericles with the
later accession of Archelaos in Macedonia he must have known
what he was doing, so either he did not care how his readers
dated the dialogue, or else – and more likely perhaps – he was
deliberately making the setting independent of historical time.[25]

On the other hand authors plainly have no licence to alter
the course of history when they are not writing fiction. The
poet W. B. Yeats was once trying to convince a colleague that
there was some good to be said for the Reformation – 'You
may say what you like, but at least you have to admit that it
led to the renaissance.' When his colleague demurred, the
poet, with a magnificent gesture of his hand, proclaimed:
'Just look at O'Brien here: he's the kind of man who would
bring down the Archangel Gabriel in full flight with a brickbat
of *fact*' – and he put a wealth of scorn, it is said, into the word
'fact'.[26] There we have poetic arrogance as bad as the arrogance
of the most extreme historicists.

A chronological approach to poetry can sometimes lead to
other kinds of misunderstanding. If a chronologist were
writing the *Odyssey* he would begin with the fall of Troy or
even with Odysseus' birth. Homer postpones his account of
the departure from Troy until his ninth Book and tells us
nothing about Odysseus' birth until his nineteenth Book.
Chronologists may find this untidy, but in fact it is more
artistic and more natural than the chronological kind of
narrative – more artistic because the epic method of going
straight *in medias res* at a critical moment is more likely to
awaken and hold a hearer's interest than a day-to-day *ab*

initio story, and more natural because in actual life we generally extend our knowledge in that way. When we first encounter notable persons or events we are absorbed in what we see of them in the present moment. Only afterwards do we look back to find out about their origins and backgrounds. Our knowledge extends backwards, not forwards.

It is important to remember, too, that the ancient Greeks considered that the past was in front of them and the future behind them, the reverse of what we now think. These are only metaphors expressing time in terms of space. But within its metaphorical limitations the ancient Greek attitude was more realistic than ours. We can see nothing in the future, except through prophecy and clairvoyance, but we can, through memory, visualize what happened to us in the past. In that way we are like people walking backwards into unknown territory trying to guess what its nature will be from what we can see at the present moment and from what we have seen in time past. The normal historical method of describing events from their origin is not necessarily better than the poets' way of describing events backwards – 'forwards' as Greeks would say – from the present to the past. And, so far as anachronism is concerned, the poet is entitled to alter time as much as to alter space. When Louis XIV asked a courtier what was the right time, the courtier is said to have replied, 'Whatever time Your Majesty desires.' Perhaps this is a fiction, but if we want to enjoy poetry at its best we had better let the poets have it, royally, that way. They are supreme lords of time and space in their own created worlds.

THE FALLACY OF STATIC MEANING

The Heracleitan – and Taoist – principle of constant change applies to poems as well as to persons and things. One can never enjoy the same poem twice. Every time one reads it, one has changed, physically, mentally and emotionally, even from day to day. Over longer intervals the change can be drastic. The *Odyssey* speaks very differently to us as children, adolescents, middle-aged and elders. We are deluded by the fact that those black marks on the white pages which stir our senses and emotions and imagination remain the same. But they have no force except in each reader's immediate experience or memory. Those who have experienced something like the indignity inflicted on Achilles by Agamemnon will understand the *Iliad*'s presentation of anger and its consequences better than those who have not. Those who have lost children in war will grieve more deeply with Priam and Hecuba. Blind men will be sorrier for Polyphemos.

At the same time the actual words of poems can, of course, change their meanings in later times. Milton's shepherd who 'under the hawthorn tells his tale' was counting his sheep, not story-telling; when Hamlet is described 'as fat and out of breath', he was fat in the old sense of sweating, not obese like Burbage the actor or Oscar Browning; when Anglicans prayed for 'indifferent justice' they meant 'impartial'. Every student knows that what Homer meant by words like *dêmos* and *areté* was not the same as what fifth-century Athenians and other Greeks meant by them. Horace sadly recognized this mutability in language when he remarked: 'As forests change their leaves with the declining years . . . so the old generation of words perishes, and those newly born blossom and flourish like young men.'[27] In that sense poems are not monuments more durable than bronze.

Further, sensitivity to human affairs varies in force and direction from era to era. In an age of pacificism certain passages in Euripides and Homer take on a sharper definition. Only recently has the strong irrational element in Greek life been brought into clearer focus. As a result, our general picture of the classical authors has distinctly changed in several respects. It will continue to change as long as these authors are actively studied. To some extent, then, we may agree with a contemporary critic of English literature when he writes:[28]

> Shakespeare has more meaning and value now than he had in his own day. There is a sense in which Homer . . .

has more meaning and is more valuable today than ever before.

But his assumption of present-day superiority may be questioned. Who of us knows for certain how much Shakespeare meant to sensitive and intelligent hearers in the Elizabethan age, or Homer to his hearers? Were, say, Marlowe and Chapman likely to have considered Shakespeare's plays less 'valuable' than did Yeats or Eliot? Can we be confident that Sophocles and Socrates found Homer less meaningful than do present-day critics and scholars? The primitivistic fallacy lurks in the background here. All we can say with fair assurance is that the meanings have certainly changed, for better or for worse.

THE FALLACY OF ALWAYS CLEARLY INTENDED MEANING

Critics generally assume that poets know exactly what they intend to say when they are composing their poems. Being methodical and precise people themselves, they expect the creative artist to be the same. The implications of the Democritan doctrine of poetic madness are against this view. Creative writing may be more like *glossolalia* than essay-writing. Poets have confessed that they were not sure what phrases meant even after they had incorporated them in a poem. Lewis Carroll once inquired from Tennyson what was the meaning of his description of a poet as 'Dowered with the hate of hate, the scorn of scorn, the love of love'. Tennyson replied that 'he was quite willing it should bear any meaning the words would fairly bear; to the best of his recollection his meaning when he wrote it was "the hate of quality of hate etc", but he thought that the meaning "the quintessence of hatred" finer'.[29]

Lewis Carroll himself, when asked what *The Hunting of the Snark* meant, replied 'I'm very much afraid I didn't mean anything but nonsense! Still you know, words mean more than we mean to express when we use them; so a whole book ought

to mean a great deal more than the writer means.'[30] Hallam
Tennyson has recorded a similar remark by his father:[31]

> The Bishop of Ripon . . . once asked him whether they
> were right who interpreted the three Queens who accom-
> panied King Arthur on his last voyage as Faith, Hope
> and Charity. He answered: 'They are right and they are
> not right. They are three of the noblest of women. They
> are also those three Graces, but they are much more. I
> hate to be tied down to say, "This means that", because
> the thought within the image is much more than any one
> interpretation.' As for the many meanings of the poem
> my father would affirm, 'Poetry is like shot-silk with
> many gleaming colours. Every reader must find his own
> interpretation according to his ability, and according
> to his sympathy with the poet.'

If the ghost of Homer could be asked whether he intended the
Odyssey to be taken allegorically as well as literally, he might
well reply like that.

A consequence of belief in clear-cut meanings is a reluctance
among critics to accept the possibility of deliberate ambiguity
in literature. I see now that in my *Ambiguity in Greek Literature*
(1939) I overstated the case for its frequency in Greek poetry.
But the main contention was, I still believe, valid, and there
is clear evidence that at least some ancient and medieval
writers deliberately exploited polysemanticism, as when Dante
expressly asserted that he intended his *Divine Comedy* to have
four distinct levels of meaning.[32]

I offer one example which poses an unanswerable critical
problem – a problem which anti-intentionalists would consider
futile to ask. When in the prophecy of Teiresias in *Odyssey* XI
Homer used the phrase *ex halós* to state how Odysseus would die,
did he recognize and intend an ambiguity between 'death
coming from the sea' and 'death off (i.e. not on) the sea'? We
shall never be able to decide this unless, miraculously, some
contemporary record of Homer's intention turns up. But
whether the ambiguity was intentional or not, its effect on
subsequent stories about Odysseus offers a spectacular example
of how an ambiguity can leave room for vast expansions.

Post-Homeric poets who took it as meaning 'death from the sea' produced an astonishing and sometimes brilliantly creative series of poems to tell just how Odysseus came to die in that way. Besides the rather pedestrian inventions in the *Telegony* and the Troy Tale, three post-classical presentations of Ulysses as setting out to wander away from Ithaca again after his Odyssean return are outstanding achievements of European literature – the twenty-sixth canto of Dante's *Inferno*, Tennyson's *Ulysses* and Kazantzakis's *Odysseia*.[33] So much could an ambiguous preposition create.

THE FALLACY OF PRIMITIVE STUPIDITY

This consists in believing that subtle thought did not exist in 'primitive' societies as, for example, in the Greek 'Dark Age' when Homer and Hesiod composed their poems. The belief is mainly based on an assumption that mental sophistication is coeval with materialistic progress – that a man who can work a computer must be more intelligent than a man who can track a wolf. We have already seen how Leaf agreed with a German editor in finding Homer's poignant comment about mourning women as 'foreign to the mind of our poet', and how the historian of the Royal Society, Bishop Sprat, urged scientific writers to 'return back to the primitive purity and shortness' of speech when 'men deliver'd so many things in an equal number of words'. Nineteenth-century confidence in the principle of progress in human society strengthened this belief in *Urdummheit*, as Murray's *Rise of the Greek Epic* has illustrated. Such a belief in consistent progress was equivalent in terms of culture and civilization to Emile Coué's mantra for optimists: 'Every day and in every way I am getting better and better.' It is the opposite of the ancient belief in continuous degeneration from a primal golden age.

Modern anthropologists have mostly come to reject this self-satisfied belief in improvement all round. As Claude Lévi-Strauss has expressed it:[34]

Prevalent attempts to explain alleged differences between the so-called 'primitive' mind and scientific thought have resorted to qualitative differences between the working of the mind in both cases while assuming that the objects to which they were applying themselves remained very much the same. If our interpretation is correct, we are led toward a completely different view, namely that the kind of logic which is used by mythical thought is as rigorous as that of modern science, and that the difference lies not in the quality of the intellectual process, but in the nature of the things to which it is applied . . .

Or, as he puts it more tersely elsewhere, 'Pre-history is nobody's childhood.'

It has always suited historicistic critics to accept a belief in primitive naivety. It helps them to decide what is 'early' or 'late' in primeval poetry, in the manner of Leaf in his *Iliad.* No one, of course, can deny that language and thought change from age to age, and that linguists and philosophers can detect these changes on the basis of firmly dated documents. The fallacy lies in the assumption that these changes are always in the direction of greater sophistication.

A variation on this fallacy is to assume that the mind of an author will develop, as he grows older, in the direction that seems best in terms of modern thought. A celebrated Platonist in our century has adequately answered this prejudice.[35]

The assumption that works in which there is a large element of semi-poetical myth must be 'juvenile' rests on another assumption, for which we have no evidence at all, that we know independently what the personal temperament of the youthful Plato was. We have only to think of the known chronological order of the work of Goethe to see how unsound a method must be which would require us to regard the second part of *Faust* or *Wilhelm Meisters Wanderjahre* as juvenile productions.

Shakespeare's *Tempest*, and perhaps the *Odyssey* – if, as 'Longinus' believed, it was the work of Homer's old age – show the same fondness for imaginative themes in late writings.

THE EGOISTIC FALLACY

Samuel Johnson, that confident critic, once had the audacity to accuse an author to his face of not knowing the correct meaning of a word in his own poem. The author was Goldsmith, the line was the first in *The Traveller*,

> Remote, unfriended, melancholy, slow.

Goldsmith when questioned whether 'slow' here meant 'tardiness of locomotion', answered 'Yes.' Johnson contradicted him. 'No, sir; you do not mean tardiness of locomotion; you mean that sluggishness of mind which comes upon a man in solitude.'[36] As is well known, Johnson was very apprehensive of such sluggishness of mind in his own case.

Classical criticism offers many examples of this kind of egoistic 'projection'. A century ago rationalists saw Euripides as a rationalist. Recently a scholar interested in parapsychology has presented him as an irrationalist.[37] Agnostics have made him an agnostic, deists, a deist, and so on.

Egoism of that kind – it can be quite unconscious – could cause even so good a Hellenist as Gilbert Murray (after his historicistic phase) to translate a passage in Euripides against the clear meaning of the Greek.[38] Being himself a gentle pacifist as well as a devoted admirer of Euripides, he apparently found it impossible to believe that the Chorus in the *Bacchai* could exclaim: 'What privilege of the gods is finer than to hold one's hand over the head of one's enemies, with superior force?' So he translated the second part of the Chorus's question as 'to hold a hand uplifted over Hate', making a pious aphorism out of a savage war-cry in a way that neither the context nor the Greek text will permit.

Murray was too good a scholar not to feel qualms about this interpretation. In a footnote he remarked, 'If I am wrong, the refrain is probably a mere cry for revenge . . . ' In fact this is just what the circumstances strongly indicate: the Chorus consists of devout maenads, who when frenzied by Dionysos would be capable of tearing animals asunder and eating their raw flesh. But Murray, misled partly perhaps by the character-as-author fallacy here, as well as by his own fervent belief in pacifism, let his improbable bowdlerization stand in his text – ironical in view of his allegations about expurgation in the Homeric poems – and thereby most probably misled tens of thousands of his Greekless readers.

THE FALLACY OF IDEAL CONDITIONS

Unlike the idealistic picture of a poet undisturbedly composing his verses in his tower or garret, or by the seashore, or on a quiet country road, the professional poets of antiquity often had to cope with very trying conditions – at banquets, festivals or competitions or public recitals where they would have to make every effort to arrest and hold turbulent and talkative audiences. If they failed to maintain interest and attention, their attempts to publish their works would be a failure. The acoustic properties of their works would need to be sonorous, and in various milieus certain subjects would have to be avoided and certain dialects would be repudiated.

Further, when poetry came to be written down in the Greek alphabet, many of the sound-effects achieved by the poet orally must have been incapable of transmission in terms of an alphabet of twenty-two or twenty-four characters. (Bernard Shaw actively campaigned for the use of an English alphabet of over forty letters.) It is totally impossible now to determine what these lost sound effects may have been. But theoretically, at least, some of the words we find in the written text of Homer may have been imposed on the poet or his scribes by alphabetical inadequacies.

A passage in the Old Testament illustrates this state of affairs. In the Hebrew version of the Book of Judges, chapter 12, certain captives are asked to pronounce *shibboleth* as a test of their tribal affinities. The Greek translators could not render the initial *sh* sound because there was no symbol for it in the Greek alphabet. (Hence the added letters in the

Slavonic alphabet.) So they could render the Hebrew word only by a paraphrase, 'the password', thereby weakening the narrative.

Vocal disabilities in a poet or orator could also affect his choice of words. If the lisping Alcibiades had written poems for recitation he would have been well advised to avoid syllables containing *r*. A modern orator, Aneurin Bevan, suffered, like Demosthenes, from a bad stammer in his youth. He searched dictionaries to find alternatives to common words which he found hard to pronounce. This, it is thought, contributed to the fresh and unusual wording of his speeches in later life.[39]

In theatrical performances difficulties of production may make it necessary to change the texts, as an amusing incident at a country performance of *Macbeth* exemplifies.[40] The producer had taken care to emphasize that a drum would be required offstage to introduce the line

A drum, a drum, Macbeth doth come.

Unfortunately at the last moment the drum could not be found. Only a flute was available. So he adroitly directed that the line should be spoken as

A flute, a flute, and here's Macbeth the brute.

Similar contingencies may well have caused less unsubtle changes in the text of Greek dramatic poetry.

Poems or works of art commissioned by a patron or patrons will obviously be subject to stronger external pressures than those in which the poet or artist is free to follow his own inclinations. The poet W. B. Yeats was chairman of the committee appointed by the government of the Irish Free State to select suitable designs for a new Irish coinage. He hoped to model it closely on Greek coins. But he soon encountered practical difficulties. Modern coins could not be stamped in high relief or be in any way asymmetrical, but 'must pitch and spin to please the gambler, and pack into rolls to please the banker'. Further, the animals depicted on the obverse had to be submitted to the Department of Agriculture for approval, and these experts on 'horse-flesh, or bull-flesh, or swine-flesh', as Yeats called them, insisted on naturalistic modifications in the formalized horse, bull or pig.[41] Fortunately Yeats was not so closely confined in his poetry.

These are the kinds of pressures that are bound to affect poets of the market-place, so to speak, in contrast with the Proustian kind of poet in his sound-proofed room. A master-poet will always overcome them. But a poet or artist who concedes too much to external pressures is likely to fail. An anecdote about Polycleitos, the great Argive sculptor of the fifth century BC, shows one way of demonstrating this danger. When visitors kept on pestering him by suggesting improvements in his latest work, he made two statues, one according to his own standards, the other embodying the suggestions of his friends. When he exhibited both of them, one was ridiculed, the other highly praised. Polycleitos told the critics: 'This one which you find so faulty is *your* work. The other is mine.'[42] If Milton or Homer had lived to hear the kind of improvements in their work that factualistic critics have suggested, they might well have drawn the same moral – 'Thank you for making my *Paradise Lost* more scientifically accurate, Dr Bentley, but that's your poem, not mine.'

THE FALLACY OF HYPERBOLE

By this I mean the belief that exaggeration is always a bad thing, not the obvious fact that hyperbole unless recognized as such is fallacious. Some commentators seem to think that poets should express their feelings and opinions in the manner that has been attributed to an English nobleman[43] – 'I should have thought that one might say that it could easily be held that . . .' Such tentativeness and modesty is commendable in scholars and critics faced with imponderable matters. But in poetry and in popular teaching other methods are needed. Jesus Christ could use very daring hyperboles at times – 'Truly I tell you that it is easier for a camel to go through the eye of a needle, than for a rich man to enter the kingdom of heaven', and 'If your eye offends you, pluck it out.' Proverbs exaggerate, presenting a frequent occurrence as an unvarying result. 'A stitch in time saves nine' (nine of course, for the sake of assonance). 'He who hesitates is lost' (then why 'Look before you leap'?) 'Faint heart never won fair lady' (masterful ladies may prefer faint-hearted gentlemen).

Poetic hyperbole is a symptom of that process of generalization which Aristotle in his *Poetics* proposed as the essence of the poetic process – that is to say, not Alcibiades as he actually was, limited in time and space and personality, but an Alcibiades-type, an extrapolated Everyman-Alcibiades. Aristotle, though a very precise scientist himself, expressed a tolerant attitude towards exaggeration in general. Referring to the pleasure that astonishment gives, he remarks, 'As a proof, there is the fact that everybody in telling a story adds on, because this gives enjoyment.'[44] In this respect the Greek people in general seem to have resembled the Irish. In terms of the legal formula 'the truth, the whole truth and nothing but the truth', the Hibernian tendency is to 'add on', to tell more than the truth, while some of the neighbouring races tend to tell less than the truth, to understate. Strictly speaking both kinds are equally mendacious, but moralists generally prefer the negative lie of understatement to the positive lie of overstatement.

THE FALLACY OF NUMBERS

This consists in taking numbers in poetry as being mathematically precise, as when efforts are made to locate places visited by Odysseus in his wanderings on the basis of the number of days apportioned by Homer to each of the stages in his voyage, or when the number of ships in Homer's 'Catalogue' are taken as historical.

Poets may choose numbers for vague effects (as in 'ten thousand times ten thousand'), or because they are proverbial (as in 'forty days and forty nights'), or because they are symbolical (especially seven and three), or because they provide the kind of sound effect that is required in a particular phrase. The last motive can be seen in the 'kisses four', which La Belle Dame Sans Merci gave to the pale knight at arms. Rhyme more than reason or passion prescribed that number. Similarly the 'nine bean-rows' of Yeats's 'Innisfree' were probably chosen for the sake of assonance and alliteration with 'arise', 'cabin', 'hive' and 'honey', rather than for horticultural reasons. Rupert Brooke in the last two lines of 'Grantchester' asked:

> Stands the church clock at ten to three
> And is there honey still for tea?

A biographer[45] has stated that in fact the Grantchester clock stood at half past three. If that was so, either Brooke's memory failed or else – and I think more probably – he discarded the historical fact in order to avoid the heavy rhythm and thick consonants of 'half past three' in favour of the lighter 'ten to three', which also gave better alliteration and assonance with 'honey' and 'tea'. Such things matter more to poets than the right time.

When the metre of poetry is strictly controlled in its arrangement of long and short (or, preferably, in the new terminology, heavy and light) syllables, certain numbers may be unusable. Homer's hexameters, for example, do not admit the Greek word for seventy (*hebdomēkonta*). The fact, then, that the number seventy does not occur in the 'Catalogue of Ships' in *Iliad* II may have resulted more from metrical necessity than from arithmetical or historical considerations.

Even so sharp a critic as A. E. Housman could accept the quantitative fallacy, it seems. Commenting on Swinburne's lines:[46]

> A table of all clear gold thereby
> Stood stately, fair as morning's eye,
> With four strong silver pillars, high
> And firm as faith and hope may be,

he observed:

> These four pillars are the four legs of the table: they were
> possibly five feet in height, probably less, certainly not
> much more: and they were as high as hope may be. Now
> therefore we know the maximum height of hope: five feet
> and a few odd inches.

It suited Housman's critical intention here – the context does
not suggest that he was joking – to treat Swinburne's lines
as if he were describing an actual table. Actually one might
as well ask, 'How high is a high hope?'

There are some works of creative literature in which one
is entitled to ask precise quantitative questions. Swift in
Gulliver's Travels took trouble to work out the measurements
of his pygmies and giants and of their worlds. But creative
authors belonging to the pre-scientific age rarely, if ever,
regarded numbers and quantities as more than impressionistic,
and ever since then poets have always considered themselves
free to adapt numbers to their poetic purposes.

In contrast with Swift's quantitative precision, Homer,
when he wants to give an idea of the huge dimensions of the
Cyclops, contents himself with remarking that his club was
the size of the mast of a twenty-oared vessel. If we knew how
tall such masts were in Homer's time, and what was the usual
proportion between a giant's club and his own height, we might
be tempted to try to estimate Polyphemos' size in feet and inches.
Fortunately we do not know that, so we escape the temptation.
Anyway, Homer's units of measurement elsewhere are vaguely
taken from stretches of the human body which could vary
considerably. (In old-fashioned haberdashers' shops where the
sellers measured a yard from their nose to their outstretched
finger-tips, a wise customer went to the tallest seller in the shop.)

To avoid the risk of being taken too literally, poets sometimes
take refuge in numerical vagueness. For large numbers the
Greeks could make an easy substitution. The word *múrios*,
'ten thousand', lost its specific reference and became 'huge
numbers, myriads' when accented *muríos*. Tennyson chose the
vague English term 'myriads' in his

> Myriads of rivulets hurrying through the lawn.

Taken literally the phrase would raise doubts about just how much lawn would be left if so many streams traversed it. But if our critical sense is lulled by the music of the rippling *r*s, we accept the line for its music and not for a clear visual image.

On one occasion a poet was persuaded to modify what looked like an extreme numerical hyperbole. This was Coleridge. Under critical pressure he changed 'a million million slimy things' in his *Ancient Mariner* to 'a thousand thousand'.[47] In fact the first quantity was justifiable in terms of marine protozoa, and the line suffered from losing its *l*-assonance.

To sum up: numbers are used by poets mainly in four ways: to state a fact or an accepted belief; to give an appearance of precision when in fact the poet has no precise information (I suspect that the numbers in Homer's 'Catalogues' and in Odysseus' voyages are of this kind); to suggest non-arithmetical associations, as in the 'mystical' use of three and seven in Rossetti's *Blessed Damozel*,

> She had three lilies in her hand,
> And the stars in her hair were seven;

and for euphonic effect, as in the examples already quoted. The commonest scholastic fallacy is to insist on the first to the exclusion of the other possibilities. In fact the only time one can trust a poet's quantifications is when they are corroborated by independent evidence.

A story about Roger Ascham shows how a similar flexibility in handling numbers can be employed for less poetical purposes. When drafting an elegantly written petition to Queen Mary for renewal of his pension, previously £10, he saw to it that the blank space in which the sum to be now granted would be inserted would be too big for the number *decem*. In presenting the document to Bishop Gardiner, his protector at court, he drew his attention to the size of the gap, which, he suggested, would nicely fit *viginti* or *triginta* or 'best of all' *quadraginta*. He also observed that it would be tedious and expensive to have the document written out again. Gardiner, amused at the ruse, went to the Queen and secured him a pension of £20.[48] Similarly for many poets a number is initially a blank space to be filled as the requirements of their poem prescribe.

FALLACIES OF METRE

Until recently most editors of classical poetry analysed the metres elaborately but paid little or no attention to the other musical elements in the diction – alliteration, assonance and pitch variation. A 'false quantity' was deemed to be one of the worst crimes that a writer or speaker could commit. But in fact what most classical scholars, in the English-speaking world at least, deemed to be a false quantity was often not a matter of quantity but of stress. The present writer still remembers with acute embarrassment how he was denounced by an elderly lecturer for pronouncing the place-name *Mŭkǎlē* as Mŭkǎlē, stressing, and perhaps slightly lengthening, the *á*. 'It's Míckaly, Míckaly, Míckaly,' the lecturer shouted. Many years later I was relieved to learn that the one thing no Greek, ancient or modern, probably ever said was 'Míckaly'. The ancient Greeks in all probability pronounced the *a* as short, unstressed, and with the high tonic accent. The modern Greeks pronounce the word more or less as I did. The lecturer's way of pronouncing it – that is, like Latin – was popularized in the late seventeenth century by the Dutch scholar H. C. Henning ('Henninius'). Unhappily English-speaking scholars accepted it *holus-bolus*. Only within the last seventy years or so has it been gradually discarded.

The main reason, of course, why metre has always been studied intensively is that it has been quantitatively analysed and classified since the fourth century BC. Terminology – as in the recent change-over from 'long' and 'short' vowels to 'heavy' and 'light' syllables – and methods of scansion have varied considerably from time to time. For that reason Jebb's edition of Sophocles and Gildersleeve's Pindar are now outmoded in matters of metre. But it must not be forgotten that the neat patterns of 'longs' or 'shorts' which teachers present to their classes when expounding the simpler metres are based on the deluding fallacy that all the vowels or syllables in Greek or Latin can be legitimately classified as units and half-units – as if a word like *sphínga* took no longer to pronounce at normal speed than *álla*, each taking exactly a beat and a half on a metronome. Actually the likelihood is that in Greek and Latin there were numberless minute gradations of length in the various syllables.

Doctrinaire metricians and dogmatic denouncers of 'false quantities' were, in their day, among the worst enemies of poetry. For fear of their scorn many a student avoided ever pronouncing Greek and Latin at all. These dogmatists, as if they were mathematicians at heart – as some of them perhaps were – seem to have been happiest when they were reducing a lyric poem to an equation of long and short marks in specious neat patterns. At the end of their analysis they could have been tempted to write QED, as at the end of a geometrical theorum. Here, they could feel, was a precision, a certainty and a finality which no merely literary prattle could give. With similar feelings an anatomist describing the bones of a skeleton to a class can rejoice that he has not to reckon with all the complications of living flesh. But at least the anatomist is not perpetuating an untruth that makes certain bones always exactly twice the length of others.

That is not to depreciate the value of metrical analyses as part of literary appreciation, provided that their basic convention about the relation of 'longs' and 'shorts' is clearly recognized as merely a convention, and provided that knowledge of a poet's rhythms is seen as being ancillary to total appreciation of his poem.

Many of the ancient critics drew attention to the other musical elements in poetry. Some critics, most eminently Dionysios of Halicarnassos, valued and discussed these non-metrical elements as important factors in poetic composition (as many modern critics and poets have done). Others, like

Aristotle, appear to have despised them as subjects for study by superior scholars and critics, regarding them as matters for attention merely by elocutionists. This depreciatory view seems still to be held by a good many contemporary classical scholars, who refer to assonantal and alliterative effects – sometimes in terms of disparagement – far less than to metre. One obvious reason for passing over these sound-patterns is that no satisfactory method of classifying sound-effects of this kind has been evolved. There is need here for a simplified notation, something like the traditional long- and short-marks of the metricians. If this were satisfactorily achieved, then with the aid of computers a readily scannable and understandable codification of a poem's full sound-effects might be feasible. Already some computer-based studies of letter-frequency in classical poems have begun to build up the necessary store of statistics.

Simply because one cannot detect regular patterns in the recurrence of certain phenomena is not a good reason for neglecting their presence. Whatever Aristotle and other critics have said about the supreme importance of metre, we should not neglect the testimony of the critics and poets who have emphasized the poetic value of the other musical elements in speech. To present classical poetry as if its words were chosen and arranged to suit metre alone, besides their conceptual function, is fallacious. Let me call two modern witnesses out of many.[49]

> Je cherche un mot (dit le poéte) qui soit: féminin, de deux syllabes, contenant P ou F, terminé par une muette, synonyme de brisure, désagrégation; et pas savant, pas rare. Six conditions – au moins.

So Paul Valéry attested. Robert Graves has said in modern terms very much what Dionysios suggested over two thousand years earlier:[50]

> 'Texture' covers the interrelations of all vowels and consonants in a poem considered as mere sound. The skilled craftsman varies the vowel sounds as if they were musical notes so as to give an effect of melodic richness; uses

liquid consonants, labials and open vowels for smooth-
ness; aspirates and dentals for force; gutturals for
strength; sibilants for flavour, as a cook uses salt. His
alliteration is not barbarously insistent, as in Anglo-
Saxon poems or Piers Plowman, but concealed by the
gradual interlacement of two or three alliterative se-
quences. He gauges the memory-length of the reader's
inward ear and plants the second pair of an alliterative
word at a point where the memory of the first has begun
to blur but has not yet faded. He varies his word-endings,
keeping a careful eye on *-ing* and *-y*, and takes care not to
interrupt the smooth flow of the line, if this can possibly
be avoided, by close correspondence between terminal
consonants and the initial consonants that follow
them . . .

THE NEVER-ONLY-ONCE FALLACY

Wilamowitz brilliantly epitomized this common belief of
classical scholars: *Einmal heisst niemals und zweimal heisst immer*:
'Once means never, twice means always.'[51] For example,
Leaf in his note on *Iliad* V, 449, remarks: 'The mention of the
"wraith" is not like Homer, nor does it appear on other
occasions when a hero is snatched away by a god.' One could
say much the same about the ghost in *Hamlet* or the ghost of
Dareios in *The Persians*. The fact is that one of the chief marks
of genius is to produce unique concepts and phrases. When we
are surprised, even astonished, at a new and unique element
in poetry or art, our response should not be 'Can this be
genuine?' but 'Here is genius at work again.'

THE ONCE-IS-TYPICAL FALLACY

Here we have the reverse of the previous type. When a scholar
is trying to establish a general rule which on theoretical
grounds he believes probable, though he can only find one
clear example of it, he may be tempted to introduce that

example as if it were one of many. To take an example which occurred in the writing of the present book. When I was first drafting the section on the fallacy of silent reading I had found only one clear case of a modern poet reproving someone for not noticing an audial clue in one of his poems. In introducing the illustratory anecdote I began to write, 'But modern poets, too, expect their audiences to be alert for latent sound-effects in their poems'. Realizing that this generalization was unwarranted, I changed it to 'But a modern poet, too, may . . .' The intelligent reader knows from such a way of introducing an example that the writer hopes and believes that this is not an isolated testimony, but a typical one. At the same time anyone who thinks that my views or the importance of sound-effects in ancient literature are wrong may object – 'He can quote only one witness to support him.'

The strictly objective way of presenting such evidence is: 'I have been able to find one witness in support of this view, namely . . .', leaving it to the reader to decide whether this one witness is typical or not. But when a writer is convinced that the general principle which he is arguing is true and important he feels bound to present his supporting illustrations in the most favourable light. He is entitled then, perhaps, to imply that he *hopes* the single piece of evidence is typical, never that he *knows* it is typical. His intention is not – or at least should not be – to deceive, but to persuade himself as well as his readers. His hope is that the solitary example is indeed one of many which he has not yet discovered. His *psyché*, as Aristotle puts it in his discussion of *paralogismós*, wants to believe it is so, just as Penelope wanted to believe that the Stranger's story about Odysseus was true, or as a prospector for gold or uranium when he has found one sample hopes that much more will follow.

Aristotle pithily warned against this fallacy when he observed: 'One swallow does not make a spring.' But in fact one swallow often shows that spring (or summer in northern latitudes) is on the way. Similarly one example may be a good indication of a general truth which may be fully established later. But it certainly is not a proof, in this book or anywhere else.

STEREOTYPE FALLACIES

We have already seen one of these exemplified in Leaf's *Iliad*, the belief that a poet cannot alter certain traditional elements in his poetry – the 'foundation which the epic poet dared not intentionally sap'. There the stereotype fallacy is directed towards the subject-matter of poetry. As regards poetic diction one finds it implied in the writings of Milman Parry (to whose insight Homeric studies owe so much). Parry implied that Homer *had* to use formulaic phrases invented by predecessors in the bardic schools, and he explained what he considered infelicitous phrasing in terms of this compulsory use of poetic clichés. No one can deny that much of Homer's language is formulaic, whether inherited or invented. But to suggest that a master-poet was incapable of using new turns of phrase when new ideas required them is improbable. It is an axiom of literary criticism that the greater the poet, the greater the originality.

Because the word 'originality' has been distorted in modern usage, that axiom may seem inept for classical poetry. The best classical poets of Greece and Rome certainly did not aim at the bizarre novelties of some modern writers. But subtly, as in Virgil's or Ovid's diction, or plainly, as in Dante's rejection of Latin for his *Divine Comedy*, every great poet is an innovator in language. Stereotypes in the sense of phrases prefabricated by others can certainly be useful in poetic composition, especially if it is oral. But they will not 'call the tune' for any except mediocre poets.

The second kind of stereotype fallacy arises when critics form their own rigid criteria for testing whether a literary work is genuine or not, as when scholars reject the authenticity of the *Prometheus Bound* because it differs so widely in style from the other extant plays of Aeschylus. Apart from the circularity

involved in this argument – it differs from all the plays tradi-
tionally attributed to Aeschylus only if one first excludes it
from the canon – by the same criterion Shakespeare's *Tempest*
and Joyce's *Finnegans Wake* and W. B. Yeats's last poems, and
indeed the later works of many scholars, would be spurious.
Again and again writers of genius have shown that it is a
supreme quality of genius to produce astonishingly uncharac-
teristic works. Further, it is particularly hazardous to use
strangeness as an indication of different authorship when only
a small portion of an author's work has survived, as in the case
of Aeschylus.

A third kind of stereotyping consists in setting up artificial
norms for literary genres and then proceeding to use them as
regulative canons. A. E. Housman refuted that view in his
inaugural lecture at Cambridge:

> No two particular things are exactly alike, and the better
> we know them the less alike we find them: perfect know-
> ledge, if we possessed it, would render generalization
> impossible. Nothing is more foolish, nothing combines
> pedantry and thoughtlessness in a more untoward union,
> than solemn prating about the laws of criticism, and
> pious horror at their violation. A man who never violates
> the laws of criticism is no critic. The laws of criticism are
> nothing but a string of generalizations, necessarily
> inaccurate . . .

Here is a simple example of the effect of critical stereotyping
as Housman defined it. The first translator of the *Odyssey* who
dared to translate Nausicaa's mode of address to her father in
Odyssey VI – *Páppa phíl'* – in equivalent nursery-language as
'Daddy dear' was that pioneer of practical methods in Greek
studies, W. H. D. Rouse, in his translation in 1938. Others
had rendered it in terms ranging from 'Honoured sire' to
'Dear father'. Their reason for avoiding the deliberately naive
flavour of Homer's phrase was presumably something like this:

> The *Odyssey* is an epic poem;
> Epic conventions preclude baby-talk;
> Therefore *Páppa phíl'* can't be accepted or translated
> as such.

(This merges into the fallacy of impropriety.)

There may, however, have been a kind of stereotype which could have helped dramatic poetry and, to a smaller degree, narrative poetry as well. The 'facts' of the main tragic themes may have been well known to Greek audiences. That it seems, was the reason why the fourth-century poet Antiphanes[52] made one of his characters complain that the tragic dramatists had an advantage over the comic writers because the audiences at a tragedy knew in advance what was going to happen to people like Oedipus, while the comic writers were expected to invent new stories for themselves.

Unfortunately for our reliance on Antiphanes' testimony Aristotle, writing later in the fourth century, states in his *Poetics*[53] that only a few people knew 'the known things' (*tá gnórima*) in traditional tragedies. Which statement are we to believe? In the past scholars generally accepted Antiphanes' remarks at their face value: audiences for the most part knew the traditional stories at least in outline. More recently, opinion, influenced perhaps by the prevailing reluctance to accept traditional forms, has veered towards Aristotle:[54] most of the audience did not know the old stories, and the speaker in Antiphanes' play was being absurd.

Perhaps the truth lies between these two opposite views. Antiphanes could have meant that the ancient myths were generally known in broad outline, while Aristotle could have meant that the details, as distinct from the broad outlines, were known only to the well-educated members of the audience. (Aristotle made a distinction elsewhere[55] between the 'liberal and educated' spectators and the 'vulgar ones' who consisted of manual workers and servants.) It seems most unlikely that even the least educated Athenian would be ignorant of the fate of figures like Oedipus and Agamemnon and Hippolytos. The tragic deed of violence and suffering – the *páthos* in Aristotelian terms – would then be fixed in the minds of all who came to see the play. But the details of how earlier poets – Homer or Hesiod or whoever – had presented the circumstances of each *páthos* would be known only to the more literate spectators.

If that were so, we must acknowledge a set of poetic stereotypes in ancient Greek literature: Agamemnon must be
murdered; Oedipus must kill his father and marry his mother;
the Trojan women must go into slavery, and so on. But apart
from this central core poets could have felt themselves free to
alter the details to suit their own artistic aims. So Aeschylus
made Clytaemnestra take the lead in killing Agamemnon,
not Aigisthos as in the *Odyssey*; and Sophocles sent Oedipus,
blind, into exile, though Homer had let him reign on in Thebes;
and, as we have seen, Homer placed Agamemnon's palace in
Mycenae, but Aeschylus transferred it to Argos.

Does this mean that Leaf was right in asserting that there
could be a foundation which a poet 'dared not intentially sap'?
No, for two reasons. First, Leaf alleged that the unsappable
foundation for Homer included details of dress and furniture
and armour and the like. Second, to use the term 'dared not'
would be misleading in the case of tragedians. It was not a
matter of not daring, it was – I believe – a matter of knowing
that it suited poetry – and dramatic poetry in particular – to
accept certain matters of faith, so to speak, which all knew
and many believed. If it had suited the major Greek dramatists
to try to overthrow the transitional version of any *páthos*, they
were free to do so. (Some authors, including Simonides and
Euripides, accepted a radically different version of the story
of Helen of Troy: there have been modern writers who alleged
that Christ was never crucified.) But by keeping to the orthodox
versions (as Socrates for different reasons did) they could work
up a much higher degree of suspense in the audience than if
the outcome of their tragedies was uncertain. Modern drama
relies mostly on curiosity and surprise: the audience is kept
wondering whether the murderer's plans will succeed or not,
and who will suffer in the end, or will no one suffer. Their
feelings are like those of someone going to consult a surgeon
about alarming symptoms in himself or in someone dear to
him – anxiety, uncertainty, and varying degrees of optimism
and pessimism, but no solid grounds as yet for pity or fear. But
when we are definitely told that we or our friend must face

a serious and painful operation within a few weeks, then what Aristotle singled out as the chief tragic emotions, pity and fear, have full scope. Similarly, a sudden unexpected disaster is at first shocking rather than pitiful and fearful. But when one hears that a disaster is inevitable and imminent the pity and fear increase according as the shock is diminished. Those who actually witnessed the assassination of President Kennedy were probably less deeply moved in terms of the tragic emotions than those who, with foreknowledge of the crucial event, saw it on a newsreel later. Foreknowledge extends the range of *páthos* backwards, giving it double power.

Foreknowledge of the *páthos* on the part of the audience gave the Greek tragedies another advantage. They could use dramatic irony freely. When one knows that Oedipus has killed his father and married his mother – while he himself and his interlocutors do not know it – his words and actions can have poignant ambiguities and overtones for those who are already informed about his future. With such prescience the audience become like gods for a while, but not having the compassionless natures of the Greek gods they suffer like Cassandras as the deeds of doom approach. Emotionally this can be much more powerful than a state of uncertainty. Ignorance about the outcome of a play or narrative may make it more 'interesting' intellectually, but to argue from that to a belief that the Greek poets and audiences would prefer themes unconstricted by tradition is – as I see it – fallacious.

It was probably for such reasons – a greater degree of suspense and greater opportunities for dramatic irony – that this particular stereotype was acceptable to the classical Greek poets and their audiences. There is no factualism involved here. The poets were not inhibited from changing the *páthos* of a traditional story by respect for 'truth'. They took over the mythical deeds of violence chiefly because their universal familiarity served the chief aim of the literary art – *psuchagogía*. If they had wanted to present Agamemnon as murdering Clytaemnestra or Ajax as killing his Greek enemies and not himself, they were free to do so – just as if they had wanted to fly they could, as I have suggested, have built aeroplanes. In both cases they chose to keep to the existing order of things, probably more through prudence than through mere conservatism.

THE FALLACY OF AUTOPSY

It is sometimes assumed that vivid descriptions of places or persons imply direct personal knowledge. Two quotations will serve as warnings against this. Anthony Trollope says in the fifth chapter of his autobiography:[56]

> I have been often asked in what period of my early life I had lived so long in a cathedral city as to have become intimate with the ways of a Close. I never lived in any cathedral city, – except London, never knew anything of any Close, and at that time had enjoyed no peculiar intimacy with any clergyman.

Archdeacon Grantly, he adds, was 'simply the result of an effort of my moral consciousness' and such as 'an archdeacon should be': in fact he had not, he believed, ever spoken to an archdeacon before he wrote *The Warden*.

Stephen Spender has said the same thing in more general terms:[57]

> I believe that, in theory, there are very few situations in life which a poet should not be able to imagine, because it is a fact that most poets have experienced almost every situation in life. I do not mean that a poet who writes about a Polar expedition has actually been to the North Pole. I mean, though, that it is possible for him by remembering imaginatively his own felt experience to know what it is like to explore the North Pole.

THE FALLACY OF RESTRICTIVE FORM

This, I believe, is a non-fallacy – the product of the libertarianism of the romantic period and of modern artistic anarchy. Many modern poets and some modern critics seem to believe that regular structure is a straitjacket. Poor Homer with all those dactyls and spondees and traditional formulae to cope with! Unhappy Sappho to have to squeeze so much passion into regular quatrains! Miserable Pindar with all that rigid strophic responsion on his hands!

In fact the nature of poetic genius is often such that it needs a firm formal structure to control it, as when James Joyce adopted Odyssean structure for his *Ulysses*. Aristotle's insistence on the importance of the plot in drama – plot with its clear beginning, middle and end, and its overall perceptible unity – is one aspect of this beneficial structuralism. He was thinking in terms of action and thought. But metre and rhyme and assonance-patterns share in the structural process. In the hands of a master-poet these exigencies of form are far from being merely restrictive. Paul Valéry has attested that the need for one particular rhyme changed the whole course of one of his poems.[58] Dryden writing on the virtues of rhyme observed: 'imagination in a poet is a faculty so wild and lawless, that, like a high-ranging spaniel, it must have clogs tied to it, lest it outrun the judgement'.[59]

Keats's 'Ode to a Nightingale' offers a probable example of the creative power of fixed form. (I say 'probable' because the inner workings of the poetic process are ultimately inscrutable.) In his seventh stanza Keats meditates, non-ornithologically, on the immortality of the nightingale. He goes on to mention occasions when its song deeply affected people in the past. Avoiding trite references to Greek mythology, he turns first to a biblical theme:

> Perhaps the self-same song that found a path
> Through the sad heart of Ruth, when sick for home
> She stood in tears amid the alien corn . . .

(There is poetic licence here: in the biblical story of Ruth there is no nightingale.)

At this point Keats's stanza-structure required three more lines, while his rhyme-scheme demanded rhymes for 'path', 'home' and 'corn'. As a result of these exigencies we have the famous romantic image:

> The same that oft-times hath
> Charm'd magic casements, opening on the foam
> Of perilous seas in fairy lands forlorn.

Without the requirements of his chosen structure this memorable passage might never have been conceived.

This attempted reconstruction of the making of these lines needs to be qualified. First I have rationalized the poetic process in a way that I have already questioned in this book. Words and ideas may come unbidden to poets and not as the result of ratiocination. The two images of Ruth and the magic casements may have come into Keats's conscious mind together in a vague form and not successively. Stephen Spender has testified that inspiration sometimes came to him as 'something still vague, a dim cloud of an idea which I feel must be condensed into a shower of words'.[60]

Second, though in the poem as we have it Ruth comes before the magic casements, she may have come after them in the poet's consciousness. If so, the formal requirements for Keats were three lines ending in rhymes for 'hath', 'foam' and 'forlorn', not the opposite as suggested above. But the note of sadness and heart-sickness has been sounding all through the ode, so that the image of Ruth is more in sequence with the previous lines, while 'magic casements' transport us into quite a new world.

The lines that follow the reference to 'fairy lands forlorn' imply, too, that Keats himself was surprised, as it were, by that phrase:

> Forlorn! The very word is like a bell
> To toll me back from thee to my sole self!

In other words his ecstatic empathy with the nightingale and the imagery its songs evoked have been dissipated in that last beautiful, but vague, romantic vision. (This weakening of poetic energy is only too well indicated in the trite phrase Keats now uses to rhyme with 'self' – 'deceiving elf'.)

Another formalistic enrichment in these lines should not be overlooked. Underlying the rhyme and reason there is a rich pattern of *o*- and *oo*- assonances, some unstressed, some stressed – 'through', 'of', 'Ruth', 'for', 'stood', 'oft', 'opening', 'of', 'word', 'to toll', 'to', 'sole', besides the rhyming 'home', 'corn', 'foam', and the repeated 'forlorn'. It would probably be too fanciful in one way, and too literal in another, to think that this echoes the notion expressed in

> Here, where men sit and hear each other groan.

But subconsciously those repeated *o*s must affect any reader who has ears to hear. And without the formal exigencies of the poem they probably would not have emerged.

I have not been able to find an equally probable example of the creative power of formalism in classical Greek or Latin poetry. On the other hand the classical poets occasionally referred to the restrictions that their metres imposed. Horace could not name the village called Equus Tuticus in his hexameters, and Martial could not put the name Earinos in his hendecasyllables.[61] (The Greeks, as Martial complained, were much more libertarian in mispronouncing words to suit their metres.) But the mere fact that some words were excluded by structural exigencies would compel poets to let their minds range over a wider field of thought. Their rhythm-schemes or assonant-patterns could serve as scaffoldings up which the poet's imagination could climb and get a wider view. Without these structural aids the modern poet is much more restricted to his initial conceptions. For example, a rhyming poet who is composing a poem about, say, a lizard will be prompted to consider possible imaginative connections with a wizard or a gizzard or a blizzard – ideas which would probably never occur to him unless his structure demanded them. He may, of course, reject these new concepts as unsuitable, and he can always keep his references to the lizard away from the ends of his lines. But his range of thought will certainly have been extended.

The risk here, of course, is that a poet will weakly

adopt jejune clichés as props for his structures, as Pope satirized.[62]

> Where-e'er you find the *cooling Western Breeze,*
> In the next Line, it *whispers thro' the Trees;*
> If *Chrystal Streams with pleasing Murmurs creep,*
> The Reader's threaten'd (not in vain) with *Sleep.*

Homer has been accused of using traditional formulae in this jejune way. But lengthy oral poetry needs architectonics, not mere tectonics. Also, it is an illusion to believe that a master-poet or a master-architect will scorn to use prefabricated materials. A celebrated monastery in Ireland, Mount Mellary, is built from materials originally shaped for a nobleman's castle. The greater liturgies of the churches are constructed from many elements belonging to earlier traditions. Or, to take an analogy from sport, a would-be champion in tennis will never succeed unless he learns what earlier champions found to be the best way of playing strokes – forehand, back-hand, lob, smash, half-volley and the rest. Having mastered the traditional technique, then the young player can let his own innate ability use it and develop it to create his own unique personal style, weaving his predecessors' strokes into triumphant new patterns and designs. Similarly a Homer or a Pindar or a Milton or a Keats will first study and imitate the technique of their most successful predecessors in the poetic art and then go on to create a champion poetry of their own. In contrast, some modern poets are like tennis-players who try to win celebrity by parading in a demonstration to demand that tennis-courts should have no lines marked on them.

THE INTENTIONAL FALLACY

An influential school of modern criticism[63] holds that it is wrong to try to discover what the intentions of writers were on the basis of their writings alone. Speculations of that kind are, they say, subjective, unprofitable, egoistic and 'romantic'. As a warning against the risk of subjectivism here Anatole

France's caustic characterization of 'intentional' critics has been quoted:[64] 'To be quite frank, the critic ought to say "Gentlemen, I am going to talk about myself, apropos of Shakespeare".'

There are, of course, such risks. But subjectivism of that kind is endemic in all speculative literary criticism, and not confined to this particular kind of speculation. Critics who condemn intentionalism usually assert that criticism should be confined to the poem itself. There should be no teleology about it, no asking of why, only of how, when and where. Study and criticism of a poem should be as 'pure' as study of a mathematical equation. Just as geologists take no account of the intentions of a divine Creator in their theories, so literary critics should confine their attention to the observable phenomena.

Obviously that is a legitimate restriction for critics and scholars to impose on themselves. But to stigmatize those who go beyond it as victims of a fallacy may itself be fallacious. Analogies between mathematics or geology on the one hand and literature on the other are faulty. Mathematical symbols and geological specimens are not charged with clues to their author's sensations and feeling as words are. An analogy with historical documents may be truer. We do not condemn historians for combing the letters and memoirs of a Napoleon or a Garibaldi to discover whether they have left subtler clues to their inner motives beneath the surface of what they explicitly say.

The ancient critics generally confined their attention to the poems alone. At times, however, the Greeks speculated about a poet's motives and intentions. Sophocles is recorded as having remarked about the dramatic art of Aeschylus that even if he did what was needful he did it without full knowledge.[65] Plato in his *Protagoras*[66] considered himself justified in making Socrates say, with reference to a poetic phrase, 'Simonides did not understand this as you understand it.' (As we have already seen, Samuel Johnson could even tell Goldsmith to his face that he, Goldsmith, misunderstood one of his own lines.)

Other classical critics, including Aristotle, implied a similar attitude when they tried to distinguish between consciously intended effects and accidental features.

THE AFFECTIVE FALLACY

This alleged fallacy lies at the opposite end of the scale poet–poem–audience from the intentional 'fallacy'. Its principle is that critics should not try to evaluate a literary work in terms of its effect on its audiences, and further, as some suggest, critics should not concern themselves at all with such effects.[67] There is a great risk here, it is claimed, of subjectivism and egoism, as with intentionalism: the critic can only too easily slip into assuming that what he himself feels is what everyone feels or should feel.

Once again it is mainly the advocates of 'pure' criticism who condemn this 'fallacy'. But the circumstances are not the same here as in the case of intentionalism. One can plainly observe the effects of poetry, especially drama, on audiences, and one can ask them personally about their feelings. As we have seen, from the sixth century onwards critics were much concerned with the power of poetry to affect people in various ways. Plato's chief indictment in his attack on poetry, and Aristotle's defensive doctrine of catharsis, are totally 'affective'. The concept of *psuchagogia* as presented by 'Longinus' and others is also essentially 'affective', too. Their theories, and ours, may be erroneous, but their aims and methods are not necessarily fallacious. A poem without a responsive audience is sterile.

THE DOCUMENTARY FALLACY

This term has become a rubber stamp for banning a kind of literary interpretation which some critics dislike. It was influentially discussed in a widely read study of Sophoclean

drama published in 1951.[68] The fallacy was defined there as
the false assumption that a literary work like Shakespeare's
Hamlet or Aeschylus' *Agamemnon* is 'a document . . . a literal
transcript of fact; that it somehow records what, at that given
time and place, an interlinked set of people said and did'.
On the contrary, it was argued, 'literature has no depth: it
operates on a thinnish crust, and there is nothing underlying
this crust', while, in contrast, any piece of fact, as recorded in
documents, 'has depth beyond depth underlying it'. For
example, in *King Lear* Lear must have had a wife – since he had
legitimate children – and she might well have had a part in
shaping her husband's character and career. But, as Shakespeare says nothing about her, it is fallacious to speculate about
a matter of that kind.

Another classical scholar[69] has re-asserted this belief that
it is fallacious to treat characters in poetry (or art) as if they
had a previous history. If one sees in a sculptural group that
one warrior out of several has no spear we should not ask
whether he had forgotten it or whether he had dropped it.
Instead we should ask why the sculptor represented him alone
as having no spear. While this scholar does not go so far as
to say bluntly that in poetry figures have no depth, he implies
that whatever an author fails to state explicitly should be
regarded as non-existent: 'The *Antigone* began with a pile of
clean paper on Sophocles' table.' In reply to that – leaving
aside the fact that we know nothing whatever about Sophocles'
methods of composition – I suggest that months or years of
thought and feeling about the main characters in *Antigone*
may have preceded Sophocles' final draft. The actual writing
down of the words may have been only the end of such a
prolonged process. Menander when asked whether he had
finished a play answered, 'I've done all the arrangement, and
I've only to add in the little lines.'[70] Similarly Racine, when
asked whether he had finished one of his tragedies, replied
(as he had worked out the plot and characterization) 'Yes, I
have only to write it.'[71] The final version of the *Antigone*
contained less than fourteen hundred lines. Are we to believe

that this was all that Sophocles ever had in mind about this theme? And are we to believe that the language of his play is never likely to contain hints and clues to what he thought and felt about its characters off-stage, so to speak?

A critic of English literature joined the attack on the documentary fallacy in an essay entitled 'How Many Children had Lady Macbeth?'[72] He rejects the remark by the novelist Hugh Walpole that 'the test of a character in any novel is that it should have existed before the book that reveals it to us began and should continue after the book is closed'.[73] Even worse, we are told, is Hartley Coleridge's advice, 'Let us put Shakespeare out of the question and consider Hamlet as a real person, a recently deceased acquaintance.'

Up to a point this warning that creative literature is not rooted in historical facts is salutary. But the belief that a work of literature has no depth behind its presentation cannot be taken as proved. Other creative artists besides Hugh Walpole have testified to the contrary. A contemporary novelist has remarked: 'I always know much more about my characters than I tell my readers.'[74] Another has said that he preferred to write about imaginary people because he did not know enough about real people.[75] Shakespeare, according to Dryden, said that he had to kill off Mercutio in the third act of *Romeo and Juliet* to prevent Mercutio killing him[76] – in other words, the dimensions of that dynamic character were expanding so fast in Shakespeare's imagination that he threatened to wreck the main plot of the play. No pasteboard hero, he!

In the light of such testimonies it is hardly true to say that literature has no depth. While its characters and concepts may have no backgrounds of fact, they can have rich backgrounds in imagination. Shakespeare may have imagined as much about Lear and Lady Macbeth or Hamlet as historians know about Messalina or Pericles. Though James Joyce took more than a quarter of a million words in his *Ulysses* to describe one day in the lives of Leopold Bloom and Stephen Dedalus, his thoughts about them and their environment were – as his letters prove – wider than that. If he had ever thought of telling their whole life story he might well have felt what Saint John so poignantly expressed at the end of his Gospel: 'there are also many other things that Jesus did: I suppose that, if every one of them were recorded, the world itself would not contain the books that would be written'.

Saint John spoke as a historian, but the same could be true of what the imagination of a genius can visualize before he writes the final version of his work. Why should a literary critic be denied the right to speculate on what that imaginative background was, when a historian is not prohibited from speculating about insufficiently documented matters of history such as the flashing of the shield at Marathon or the reason why Euripides went into exile? When historians speculate about matters of that kind, no one condemns them for being deceived by a fallacy, whatever the probability or improbability of their speculations may be.

In other words, both historical texts and literary texts are documents whose backgrounds lie in various depths of obscurity. It is fallacious to restrict the term document – which essentially means a written statement offering evidence of something - to records of the factual world and to deny it to records of a writer's imagination. The ancient metaphor of 'the path of song' implies that the poet's task can be identified with that of an explorer finding a way through a dense jungle teeming with exotic plants and life. The explorer, if he is speeding on his way, does not stop to observe and describe much of what he glimpses around him. He confines himself to describing significant landmarks to help those who follow him in finding their way. In a similar fashion the poet cuts a clear and continuous pathway – narrow in lyrics, broad in dramas and epics – through a mass of imagined material, recording only what will give relevant pleasure and guidance to his followers. In making the pathway the poet has seen much more than he will tell. He has removed obstacles which subsequent travellers will not encounter. But the language and imagery he uses in what he chooses to describe may contain clues to some of what he has omitted. If that is so, critics are entitled to look for these clues and to try to interpret them correctly, bearing in mind Shelley's words: 'the most glorious poetry that has ever been communicated to the world is probably a feeble shadow of the original conception of the poet'.[77]

THE FALLACY OF OVER-VISUALIZATION

Readers of poetry can be divided into two classes: those who are more responsive to visual suggestions and those who respond better to auditory suggestions. The ideal reader is responsive to both, but for some readers visual imagery distracts them from auditory sensations and vice versa. (My impression from teaching students is that the visualizers are commoner than what I shall call the audializers, but I may be wrong.) Some readers are also sensitive to tactile suggestions.[78] (Homer spoke of 'woolly' screams, and Dante described words as 'shaggy' or 'hairy'.) A few critics have even accepted the possibility of suggestions of taste and smell from words.[79] But these alleged tactile, gustatory and olfactory sensations are primarily kinaesthetic, as will be exemplified in the next section, and not as direct as the visual and auditory sensations.

The same distinction can be made among authors. Swinburne and Poe are very much audializers. Donne, Coleridge and Pindar are preponderantly visualizers. Shakespeare, Pope, Homer and Aeschylus are masters of both media, though visualization is generally stronger in their work, as in all intellectual literature. Sight and imagery, as ancient critics recognized, are the main instruments of thought. Sound is more emotional and more sensuous.

Over-visualization occurs when a hearer or reader pays excessive attention to the physical implications of a term or phrase in literature. In the *Frogs*[80] Dionysos is, I think, guilty of it when he mocks a phrase in Euripides, 'the foot of time', as if it personified Time as having big feet, like the comic policeman in popular modern humour. If one takes 'foot' here in a general sense of 'stride' or 'pace' instead of visualizing a whole picture of Time the phrase is permissible enough. On the other hand even moderate visualizers are likely to find comic incongruity in lines such as[81]

> Love's feet are in his eyes

and

> No more will I endure Love's pleasing pain,
> Nor round my heart's leg tie his galling chain.

A clear line of demarcation cannot be drawn here. Each reader will have different thresholds of toleration for such imagery. Is Aeschylus' notorious description of the dust on a herald's clothes a tolerable 'conceit' or not? – 'mud's sister and neighbour, thirsty dust',[82] so scathingly parodied in A. E. Housman's *Fragment of a Greek Tragedy*. But figures of speech based on human relationships were so common in Greek poetry that few hearers of the messenger's phrase in the *Agamemnon* are likely to have visualized a thirsty sister there.

Censure on mixed metaphors may be the result of over-visualization. Shakespeare's lines[83]

> Was the hope drunk
> Wherein you dress'd yourself? hath it slept since
> And wakes it now, to look so green and pale
> At what it did so freely?

might be criticized for introducing the notion of dressing oneself in a lively personification of Hope. But if the lines are heard or read at the speed of a dramatic performance, 'dress'd' should not give offence. Here for a fraction of a second our minds are given a glimpse of Macbeth putting on Hope as armour or as a garment, while Hope itself is being portrayed like a person who gets drunk and sleeps and grows pale. Provided we do not let 'dress'd' take on too clear and too expansive a meaning, its momentary intrusion into the main image need not be disturbing. The camera, to use a metaphor from film-making, turns for the briefest of times from Hope to Macbeth under the influence of Hope, and then back again to the failures of Hope.

In 'mixed metaphors' of this kind one should recognize a difference in visual imagery between a visual image which presents a clear picture of an object, and one which is intended more to arouse a complex network of associations.[84] Take the cicada in Greek poetry, for example. As an insect it has no visual beauty or charm and the sound it makes is harsh and strident (though the ancient Greeks seemed to have liked it). On the other hand, for those familiar with its haunts, the mention of a cicada evokes the pleasure of the Mediterranean countryside in sun-drenched summer weather. Consequently while a blunt statement that a cicada is a charming creature would properly provoke objection, to imply the same in a symbolical reference would probably win general acceptance even from strong visualizers and audializers.

Certainly there are times when even a master-poet cannot be absolved from negligence in the use of visual imagery. Tennyson in his poem on the martyrdom of Saint Stephen wrote:

> But looking upward, full of grace,
> He pray'd, and from a happy place
> God's glory smote him in the face.

Nothing, except perhaps an almost mystical disregard for lowlier meanings of a phrase, can excuse that kind of incongruity – especially in a meditative lyric poem and not in a fast-moving drama.

Over-visualization can be detrimental to the proper enjoyment of scenes in literature as well as of figures of speech. Aristotle implies this in a passage of his *Poetics* where he is describing the pleasure of 'astonishment' or 'wonder' (*tò thaumastón*). A contemporary critic of the Zoilan school, Megakleides,[85] censured the line in *Iliad* XXII where we are told that Achilles restrained the Greek army from joining in the pursuit of Hector by nodding at them. 'How could Achilles turn back so many myriads with a nod?', asked Megakleides in scorn. Aristotle defends the line on the grounds that incidents which would not be feasible or acceptable when enacted visually, as in drama, can be successful in narrative poetry. He does not specifically speak of over-visualization, but that is the implication here. In fact a normal reader of this fast-moving episode has his attention so strongly concentrated on the fateful figures of Achilles and Hector in the foreground that the numbers and locations of the Greek army do not concern him at all. But the bookman critic, at leisure in his study, stops and over-visualizes.

THE FALLACY OF OVER-AUDIALIZATION

This uncouth term may perhaps be permitted for the sake of correspondence with 'over-visualization'. The fallacy consists in believing that one can hear and should hear literary sound-effects which in the opinion of sensible critics are not there at all. Here, as with questions of visualization, objective norms of judgment cannot be satisfactorily established. All depends on the sensitivity or hypersensitivity of each person to the auditory qualities of words.

A prejudice has to be reckoned with in this contest for priority between sight and sound. Both Plato and Aristotle regarded the auditory aspects of poetry as unworthy of consideration by high-minded literary critics, and some modern scholars and critics have expressed the same scorn. It is bound up with the belief that all images are visual in origin: in Addison's words, 'We cannot indeed have a single image in the fancy that did not make its first entrance through the sight.'[86] This must be untrue if we can believe the testimonies of many poets that ideas and images have come to them from non-visual sources. T. S. Eliot emphasized this in his far-reaching essay on the music of poetry: 'I know that a poem, or a passage of a poem, may tend to realize itself first as a particular rhythm before it reaches expression in words, and that this rhythm may bring to birth the idea and the image'.[87] Goethe, Schiller, Baudelaire, Mallarmé and others have said much the same.[88] If we neglect the audial aspects of poetry we may be neglecting not, as some imply, a few phonetic tricks and garnishings but the very root of a poem's inspiration. But certainly there is a constant risk that keen audialists may overvalue the general importance of the phonetic element in poetry. Since the present writer has been interested in this aspect of poetry for many years, the immediately following pages may be judged to contain examples of this fallacy of over-audialization.

THE FALLACY OF SILENT READING

The fact that in modern times readers generally read to themselves in silence, using the eye alone to inform the brain, tends to reinforce the notion that poetry is like painting in being a matter of seeing, not of hearing: the eye conveys the message of the words directly to the brain as it does when scanning a picture.[89] But in classical antiquity literary works were normally read aloud even by readers who were reading for themselves alone, as is attested as late as the end of the fourth century AD by Saint Augustine's surprise at finding Saint Ambrose reading a book silently.

In other words modern readers are inclined to think of the physical material of a poem as being a series of significant black marks on white pages. But for poets and readers in antiquity the physical substance of poetry was sound-waves, which in private reading were caused by the reader himself and in public performances by the actors or reciters. The alphabetical marks on the page were essentially indications of sounds. The meaning emerged when these sounds impinged on the eardrums of the auditor or auditors. The letters 'spoke' – a frequent metaphor in ancient Greek – to the reader, in contrast with earlier picture-writing, hieroglyphics and ideograms in which the message was conveyed pictorially.

Since, then, the physical material of classical poetry was sound-waves – as literally as the material of the Parthenon was Pentelic marble and the material of Greek pottery was clay – it follows that sound-effects are likely to have been much more important for the classical poets than they are for poets in the age of silent reading. No doubt it would be an exaggeration to say that to read the *Iliad* without hearing it is the same as reading a musical score without hearing the music, since music is composed almost entirely for purely musical effects, and poetry is usually intended to convey images and ideas as well. But sometimes poetry approximates to pure sound. The croak of the frogs and the cries of the birds in Aristophanes' *Frogs* and *Birds* carry no visual implications, nor does Nash's

> Cuckoo, jug-jug, pu-we, to-witta-woo,

nor Shakespeare's

> With a hey and a ho, and a hey nonino,

nor Tennyson's

> 'Tirra lirra', by the river
> Sang Sir Lancelot,

nor the shattering exclamations – *oimoi, aiai, appapai, otototoi* and the rest – uttered by tragic victims in their moment of agony. Unless the reader hears expressive words of that kind for himself, their effect is sadly diminished, as it is diminished by translators who render the almost-animal cries of a Philoctetes or Cassandra with cool cerebral phrases like 'Ah woe'.

The poets of antiquity, knowing that their poems would always be heard, could exploit these sound-effects and others of a subtler kind – subdued onomatopoeia, assonance-patterns, rhythm-variations – with much more confidence than modern poets can. But a modern poet, too, may expect his audience to be alert for what poetry can convey by its sound alone, as an anecdote about Tennyson shows. He was reading *Maud* to a young woman. After reading

> Birds in the high Hall-garden
> When twilight was falling
> Maud, Maud, Maud, Maud,
> They were crying and calling,

he asked her what bird she thought he meant. She guessed a nightingale. This made Tennyson so angry that he nearly flung her to the ground. 'No, fool!', he exclaimed ' . . . rook!'[90] She had failed to hear the recurrent *aw* sounds and the final caw in 'calling'.

That was a rather unsubtle demonstration of how important it can be to hear the sound of poetry that is intended to be heard. All poetry of that kind is likely to contain similar effects. For example when Achilles' tutor Phoenix in *Iliad* IX describes how, when he fed the hero as an infant, the child would often *apo-blúzein* the wine that he was given to drink. The verb, together with its uncompounded form *blúzein*, is generally translated 'to cause to gush out, to spurt out'. But if one pronounces the *blú* syllable properly the movement indicated is rather that of making liquids bubble out from the lips (compare English 'blubber-lip' and 'bubble') – a commonly observable gesture among infants and quite distinct from spurting or gushing.

In this example it should be noted that the mimetic force of the word lies more in the muscular movements required to pronounce it properly than in the sound of the word. This kind of mimesis – not a widely recognized one – may be called kinaesthetic onomatopoeia. It is especially effective in expressing processes which do not involve noticeable sounds, such as the word for honey, *méli* (Latin *mel, mellis*; French *miel* etc.). This word if pronounced adequately makes the lips and tongue go through the motions of tasting honey, just as Homer's word for thick cream, *glágos*, suggests gulping movements as well as glugging sounds. All such embodiments of meaning – rather than descriptions – are likely to be lost if one reads poetry silently.

Something much more important may be lost, too. 'Longinus' asserts that the emotional effect of poetry's word-music resembles that of pipes and lyres which can strongly excite the emotions.[91] In the same way, he believes, the varying speech-melodies and rhythms of poetry and oratory convey the emotions of a poet or orator right into the souls of his listeners, bewitching them and disposing them to feel a sense of grandeur, dignity and sublimity, when the poetry and oratory are of that nature, 'taking hold not just of the hearing but of the soul itself'. This *psuchagogia*, as we have seen, was regarded as the primary function of poetry by some ancient critics. If 'Longinus' is right, it will be greatly weakened when the poem is not actually heard. The intellectual content which we gain from silent reading will not provide it by itself. Here one is reminded of T. S. Eliot's challenging remark that the conceptual meaning of poetry is like the piece of meat that a burglar throws to the watchdog to keep it occupied while he goes about his proper business.

Some scholars and critics hold that it is sufficient to hear the sound of poetry in one's 'inner ear'. Just what such silent hearing means is hard to determine. It is a genuinely physical experience resulting from vestigial movements of the vocal organs? Or is it a matter of vivid imagination? A. E. Housman, who as we have seen was a strong advocate of poetic musicality, distinguished between two kinds in his essay on Swinburne. He found a difference between poets like Swinburne and Pope who in choosing their word-music 'address themselves frankly and almost exclusively to what may be called the external ear', and others like Blake and Milton whose melodies are 'addressed to the inner chambers of the sense of hearing, to the junction between the ear and the brain'. To read the first kind of poem aloud is a pleasure and delight, 'But there, in that very fact, you can tell that their music is only of the second order'. In contrast it is 'not a pleasure but an embarrassment' to read aloud poets whose music is of the first order: 'No reader can hope to do them justice . . . You should either hire an angel from heaven to read them to you, or let them read themselves in silence'.[92]

Most readers would, I think, agree that Swinburne's word-melodies are often too obtrusive. Like an over-loud musical accompaniment to a song they obscure rather than illuminate the conceptual meaning. True master-poets avoid such a conflict. But disagreement with Housman is likely to arise when he rates the poetry whose music is best heard by 'the external ear' as inferior to the poetry whose music should be read aloud only when an angel could be found to read it. Keats, it is true, had said much the same thing in his 'Ode on a Grecian Urn' – 'Heard melodies are sweet, but those unheard/ Are sweeter.' But Keats in that particular poem was bent on eulogizing the effect of the visual arts. Elsewhere he insisted on the importance of audible sound-effects in poetry.

Housman's pronouncement amounts to this: he preferred the more delicate type of word-music in poetry and generally preferred the pleasures of the inner ear to that of actual hearing. But he was writing about modern poetry which the reader can savour in the quietness of his library or study. Most of classical poetry had to be heard in quite different conditions – in the hurly-burly of a festival, or in the hubbub of a banquet, or to a lively audience in a theatre. A stronger word-music would be needed there, and a stronger music was in fact provided by the classical poets.

Other scholars who admit the importance of the acoustic elements in classical poetry sometimes object to reading it aloud because of uncertainties of pronunciation. I have written elsewhere at some length about this attitude, which I respect but reject. I shall confine myself, briefly, to two points. First, whatever may be dubious about the details of ancient Greek pronunciation, it is well established that the general tone in which it was spoken was not that of normal conversation, but something intermediate between song and conversation. (We must remember the name for all poetry before the fifth century – *aoidé*, 'song'.) Paul Valéry has affirmed that this is the best intonation for speaking modern poetry:[93]

> in studying a piece of poetry to be spoken aloud, one should never take as a beginning or point of departure ordinary discourse or current speech, and then rise from the level of prose to the desired poetic tone; on the contrary ... one should start from song, put oneself in the attitude of the singer, tune one's voice to the fullness of musical sound, and from that point descend to the

slightly less vibrant state suitable to verse. It seemed to me that this was the only way to preserve the musical essence of poems. Above all, one should *place* the voice well, as far from prose as possible, study the text from the point of view of the attacks, modulations, and sustained notes that it contains, and gradually reduce this tendency, which will have been exaggerated at first, to the proportions of poetry.

Second, it is strange but true that even when Greek poetry is read with a highly erroneous pronunciation it can have a moving and memorable effect provided that it is spoken with verve and feeling. The intoxicated student whose recitations from Homer helped to inspire the young Schliemann to go and find Troy probably used the Reuchlinian pronunciation. Very likely, too, the schoolmaster who so strongly affected C. S. Lewis in his youth used the equally unauthentic Henninian way of speaking Greek. Yet[94]

> Every verse he said turned into music on his lips: something midway between speech and song. It is not the only good way of reading verse, but it is the way to enchant boys; more dramatic and less rhythmical ways can be learned later. He first taught me the right sensuality of poetry, how it should be savoured and mouthed in solitude.

'Right sensuality' – it is an apt and memorable phrase, in full consonance with the anti-puritanical tradition of literary criticism from Democritos to Wordsworth, for the special enjoyment that comes from poetry when it recovers its living voice.

This black-list could be extended indefinitely. The allegorical fallacy – believing that allegorical meanings are intended where in all likelihood they are not – has already been noticed on earlier pages, and the 'mirror-to-nature' fallacy. Attention has been drawn in a recent book on Greek tragedy to the 'propaganda fallacy'[95] based on 'the supposition that a Greek tragedy was primarily or significantly shaped by a desire to promote a certain line on a specific contemporary issue (in politics or philosophy or whatever)'. And there is what might be called the 'irony fallacy' through which scholars, like the interpreters of dreams, hold that a statement which contradicts their theories may be interpreted as meaning the opposite of what it plainly says. But these hardly need detailed consideration.

Chapter Seven

The Freedom of Poetry

Looking back over the preceding chapters I see that I may have over-emphasized the inspirational and irrational elements in poetic composition at the expense of its more rational features – *manía* more than *téchne*, *ingenium* more than *ars*, the poet as a madman and a dreamer more than the poet as a thinker and a craftsman. My intention was to redress an over-emphasis in the opposite direction among modern classical scholars and critics, who, ignoring Aristotle's insistence on the autonomy and uniqueness of poetry, treat it as a branch of some subject that interests them more.

Perhaps, too, I have over-emphasized the non-factuality of poetry, in an effort to break the stranglehold of the historicists. Obviously poems will differ greatly in their degree of factuality. One naturally expects to find a closer approximation to history in Shakespeare's *Julius Caesar* or Aeschylus' *Persians* than in Spenser's *Faerie Queen* or Carroll's *Hunting of the Snark*. But as Aristotle explains in his *Poetics*, the reason why poets choose to write about historical personages and events is not because they want to improve our knowledge of history, but because the use of historical names gives credibility to their fictions. Unquestionably such poems will often contain verifiable historical facts. But unless their authors universalize their themes and adapt them to the requirements of the poetic art, the result will be failure. In other words titles like *Julius Caesar* or *The Persians* cause a kind of *paralogismós* in the minds of their audiences, causing them to accept the reality of the poem more readily. (But there is no evidence that Homer intended his psychological poem about the wrath of Achilles to be called the *Iliad*: this title is first used by a historian, Herodotos.)

In other words, poets cannot serve two masters, art and actuality. That was the unanimous belief of both the enemies and the friends of poetry in antiquity from Xenophanes to 'Longinus'. The 'reality' of poetry is quite different from the 'reality' of history or philosophy. A contemporary critic has expressed this admirably in a discussion of the Homeric poems:[1]

> Delight in physical existence is everything to them . . . they bewitch us and ingratiate themselves to us until we live with them in the reality of their lives; so long as we are reading or hearing the poems, it does not matter whether we know that all this is only legend, 'make-believe'. The oft-repeated reproach that Homer is a liar takes nothing from his effectiveness, he does not need to base his story on historical reality, his reality is powerful enough in itself, it ensnares us, weaving its web around us, and that suffices him. And this 'real' world into which we are lured exists for itself, contains nothing but itself; the Homeric poems conceal nothing, they contain no teaching and no secret meaning.

To highly imaginative or intensely artistic people this fictional reality can be truer and more convincing than anything that the matter-of-fact world can offer. We have already seen examples of this in the visionary experiences of Yeats and Blake as opposed to ordinary perceptions. An Irish folktale illustrates this contrast further.[2] Saint Patrick, it relates, was trying to convert the pagan Irish hero Oisín (Usheen) to Christianity. He found it hard going. Oisín was obdurate in preferring the proud heroic way to the way of Christian humility. One thing, however, made Patrick hopeful: Oisín insisted that he and his companions valued the truth and always spoke truthfully. Later a day came when Oisín complained about his daily ration of food – a quarter of beef, a churnful of butter and a round of griddle-bread. 'In the good old days', he told Patrick, 'I've often seen a quarter of a blackbird bigger than that quarter of beef, and a mountain-ash berry as big as that churnful of butter, and an ivy-leaf as big as that round of bread.'

Patrick was grieved at this apparent lie and reproved Oisín for it. Oisín resolved to show Patrick that the remark was true. After making elaborate preparations he went to a lonely valley and blew a magical trumpet there. Soon flocks of enormous blackbirds flew down. With the help of a young lad and a fierce dog he killed one of them. Its quarter was bigger than any quarter of beef, and in its belly were a huge berry and a colossal ivy-leaf. Oisín brought these back and showed them to Patrick, saying, 'You know now, Patrick of the Bells, that I told no lie; and that is what kept us all through our lifetime – truth that was in our hearts, and strength in our arms, and fulfilment in our tongues.' 'Indeed you told no lie', Patrick replied. Plainly the sympathy of the story-teller, though doubtless a Christian by profession, was with the Celtic magician-hero; not with the matter-of-fact Roman Briton.

In that way Oisín demonstrated his freedom from factuality and actuality by means of magic, just as the poet demonstrates it in terms of creative imagination. But while the technique of magic can be taught and learned, poetry, as Edmund Spenser claimed,[3] is

> no arte, but a divine gift and heavenly instinct not to be gotten by laboure and learning, but adorned with both and poured into the witte by a certain *enthousiasmos* and celestiall inspiration.

Here, in the phrase 'poured into the witte', one can find an echo of Plato's metaphor of a gushing fountain describing the spontaneity of poetic inspiration. It recurs again in Wordsworth's famous definition of poetry as 'the spontaneous overflow of powerful feelings'. Wordsworth introduced it in connection chiefly with lyrical poetry. But even such poems as the *Iliad* and *Aeneid* would have failed, as both Aristotle and Horace imply, unless their poets had themselves deeply felt the emotions of their characters. 'If you wish me to weep at your poems', Horace advised, 'you must first weep yourself.'[4] And Aristotle just before his statement that a poet must be either a person of high natural gifts or else a madman, remarked that the most persuasive poet is the one who has felt the storms of passion and anger in himself.[5]

Many modern poets have insisted on the two elements of spontaneity and emotionalism in the inspirational phase of poetic composition. Here is Robert Frost:[6]

> A poem is never a put-up job, so to speak. It begins as a lump in the throat, a sense of wrong, a homesickness, a lovesickness. It is never a thought to begin with. It is at its best when it is a tantalizing vagueness. It finds its thought and succeeds, or doesn't find it and comes to nothing.

Similarly A. E. Housman in his essay on the name and nature of poetry spoke from his own experience when he described the passivity of the poet's mind when inspiration comes to him:

> I think that the production of poetry, in its first stage, is less an active than a passive and involuntary process; and if I were obliged, not to define poetry, but to name the class of things to which it belongs, I should call it a secretion; whether a natural secretion, like turpentine in the fir or a morbid secretion, like the pearl in the oyster.

He went on to place the source of 'the suggestions to the brain' which came to him in moments of inspiration as 'the pit of the stomach' (which is lower down than the *phrénes* where classical poets located the physical origin of their poetry). In much the same way Robert Graves has described the poet's state of mind at the beginning of a poem as 'a trance-like suspension of his normal habits of thought'.[7] Blake went so far as to say that he wrote his *Milton* 'from immediate Dictation . . . without Premeditation and even against my Will'.[8] Keats remarked that he had often not been aware of the beauty of some of his thoughts or expressions until after he had written them down: they had then 'struck him with astonishment and seemed rather the production of another person than his own'.[9] Here we are back again to a belief in some kind of Muse.

According to such testimonies – and many others could be

quoted in support – poetic inspiration is far from being a rational and orderly process. But on the other hand there is no doubt that the second phase of poetic composition, the 'polishing', is largely a technological process which can be taught and learned systematically and logically – hence all those *Poetics* from Aristotle's onwards. As Shelley asserted in his *Defence of Poetry*, 'The functions of the poetic faculty are two-fold, by one it creates new material of knowledge and power, by the other it engenders in the mind a desire to reproduce and arrange them according to a certain rhythm and order which may be called the beautiful and the good.' Yet it must be remembered that inspiration can occur at any stage in the making of a poem, though it is at the beginning that its impetus is strongest. Stephen Spender has emphasized the power of words, apart from their meaning, to open up new poetic vistas: 'Sometimes when I am writing the music of the words I am trying to shape takes me far beyond the words.'[10] What happens in such cases, it seems, is like the free association which psychoanalysts use with their patients.

As we have seen, the earliest poetic freedom to be challenged and denounced by critics was their freedom to tell 'lies'. This freedom has always been the crux of the 'ancient quarrel' between the philosophers and the poets and the modern conflict between the 'two cultures' of science and the arts. As long as each side strives to impose its standards and principles on the other, agreement will never be reached between them. The scientist will demand conformity with the observable facts of the phenomenal world. The poet will continue to create his own world. To add one further example of poetic non-factuality to those quoted in previous chapters: in 'The Burial of Sir John Moore at Corunna' by Charles Wolfe, a poem famous enough to be included in Palgrave's *Golden Treasury*, it is stated that the burial took place

By the struggling moonbeam's misty light.

But in later years an astronomer[11] who checked the phase of the moon for 16 January 1809 found that the moon was not

Abbreviated References

ABRAMS   M. H. Abrams, *The Mirror and the Lamp* (Oxford, 1953).
COLLINGWOOD   S. D. Collingwood, *Life and Letters of Lewis Carroll* (London, 1898).
D–K   H. Diels and W. Kranz, *Die Fragmente der Vorsokratiker*, 10th ed., 3 vols (Berlin, 1960–1).
DODDS   E. R. Dodds, *The Greeks and the Irrational* (Berkeley, 1951).
FROST, *Letters*   Robert Frost, *Selected Letters*, ed. Lawrence Thompson (London, 1965).
GRAVES   Robert Graves, *The Common Asphodel* (London, 1949).
HARDING   Rosamond A. Harding, *An Anatomy of Inspiration*, 3rd ed. (Cambridge, 1948).
HARRIOTT   Rosemary Harriott, *Poetry and Criticism before Plato* (London, 1969).
HOUSMAN, 'SWINBURNE'   A. E. Housman, 'Swinburne', *The Cornhill*, 1061 (autumn 1969), pp. 382–400.
LOWES   John Livingston Lowes, *The Road to Xanadu* (Boston, 1955).
PRESS   John Press, *The Fire and the Fountain* (London, 1966).
Sound of Greek   W. B. Stanford, *The Sound of Greek* (Berkeley, 1967).
SPENDER   Stephen Spender, *The Making of a Poem* (London, 1955).
TAPLIN   Oliver Taplin, *Greek Tragedy in Action* (London, 1978).
Tennyson   Hallam Tennyson, *Alfred Lord Tennyson: a Memoir by his son*, 2 vols (London, 1897).
VALÉRY, *Art*   Paul Valéry, *The Art of Poetry*, trans. Denise Folliot (New York, 1958).
WIMSATT, *Icon*   W. K. Wimsatt, *The Verbal Icon* (University Press of Kentucky, 1954).
WIMSATT, *Leopards*   W. K. Wimsatt, *The Day of the Leopards* (University Press of Kentucky, 1958).

Notes

CHAPTER ONE   ENEMIES OF POETRY

1 H. J. Rose, *Handbook of Greek Mythology*, 6th ed. (London, 1958), p. 7.
2 Quoted by Douglas Bush, *Science and English Poetry* (New York, 1950), p. 40.
3 607b; cf. Plutarch, *Moralia*, 1086e–1087a.

CHAPTER TWO   HISTORICISTS

1 *A History of Greece* (1888 ed.), I, pp. 401–2 (cf. p. 435).
2 *Theogony*, 27, with West's note *ad loc.*, and Harriott, pp. 35–6 and 112–13.
3 Frag. 21 in E. Diehl, *Anthologia Lyrica Graeca*, 3rd ed. (Leipzig, 1949), vol. 1.
4 II, 110 and 120.
5 I, 9, 4 and 10, 3.
6 See further in chapter Six.
7 Boswell's *Life* (1783), chapter lvi.
8 382d; *Phaidros*, 229.
9 *Poetics*, 1451b 11.
10 1460a 18–20.
11 See Strabo, IX, 3, 11–13, where he is criticized for violating his own principles on myths; Polybios, II, 56, cf. IV, 40; Diodoros, I, 2; Pausanias, *passim*.
12 Livy, I, Preface; Quintilian, X, 1, 31.
13 Grote, *Westminster Review*, 5 (April 1826), pp. 269 ff.
14 References to Homer: *Iliad* I, 1; II, 671 ff., 484 ff. *Odyssey* I, 1; XXIV, 60–1; VIII, 62–74; XXII, 347–8; VIII, 491; XXII, 330.
15 References to Hesiod: *Theogony*, 38; 31–2; 55; 98–103. For a full discussion of the very controversial question of the function of the Muses see Harriott, chapters 1–3. (She emphasizes the element of memory.) Pindar, *Olympians*, X, 3–6 and 12–13 distinguishes between 'the Muse' and 'Truth'.
16 See further in chapter Four.
17 534a, cf. *Phaidros*, 245a; *Poetics*, 1455a 32 (see Gudeman's note); *Rhetoric*, 3, 7, 11.
18 Cf. Harding, p. 33.
19 *Two Cheers for Democracy* (London, 1951), p. 123. Cf.

Shakespeare, *Timon of Athens*, I, 1, 20–5, where the Poet compares poetry to 'a gum which oozes From whence 'tis nourish'd'. And on the Muse cf. John Updike in *Museums and Women* (London, 1973), p. 164. 'Is not the Muse a mermaid whose slippery-scaled body pops from our arms the moment we try to tighten our embrace?'

20 See further in chapter Four.

21 I am indebted to Judith Rosner for information about Lucan's fictions. For many examples of similar 'improvements' on historical fact see chapter 14 of *Heroic Poetry* by C. M. Bowra (London, 1952). The lapse by Graham Greene quoted in my next paragraph is taken from *Encounter* for January 1970, p. 92.

22 See the first edition (Oxford, 1907), pp. 1, 130, 163, 185, 181, 183, 188, 212 ff., 222, 225.

23 See his *Studies in the Odyssey* (Oxford, 1914), pp. vi, vii, 29 ff., 48 ff., 59.

24 For the following quotations see pp. vii, 9, 184, 191, 272.

CHAPTER THREE SCIENTISTS, PSYCHOLOGISTS AND MATHEMATICIANS

1 Diogenes Laertius, *Plato*, 3, 5: cf. Aelian, *Varia Historia*, 2, 30.

2 Mary Colum, *Life and the Dream* (London, 1947), pp. 165–6. The details of the scene as related by C. P. Curran in *Under The Receding Wave* (Dublin, 1970), p. 93 are quite different, but the basic contrast between the poet and the scientist is the same – another example of the fluidity of contemporary testimony.

3 *A Vision of the Last Judgment*, last paragraph.

4 In the essay entitled 'The Enchanted Woods'.

5 A. R. Michelson quoted by Theodore H. Savory, *The Language of Science* (London, 1967), p. 137.

6 Collingwood, p. 199.

7 Hecataios, frag. 1 in F. Jacoby, *Die Fragmente der Griechischen Historiker* (Berlin, 1923); Xenophanes, D–K, i, frags 11–12; Hippias, *Poetics*, 1461a 22.

8 B-scholia on *Iliad*, XVIII, 489; cf. *Poetics*, 1461a 21.

9 *Clouds*, 135 ff., *Birds*, 992 ff., *Frogs*, 797–802.

10 See H. V. Apfel, 'Homeric Criticism in the Fourth Century', *Transactions of the American Philological Association*, 69 (1938), pp. 245–58.

11 I, 3, 18.

12 *The Letters of A. E. Housman*, ed. Henry Maas (London, 1971), p. 39. Cf. Harold Nicolson, *Diaries and Letters 1930–1938*, ed. Nigel Nicolson (London, 1966), on 26 September 1931.

13 See R. Pfeiffer, *History of Classical Scholarship* (Oxford, 1968), p. 226.

14 *Idyll* 1, 72.
15 Athenaeus, *Deipnosophists*, II, 61c.
16 pp. 40, 111–12, 414, 43.
17 *A Discourse of Ecclesiastical Politie* (London, 1671), pp. 74–6.
See further in Abrams, pp. 285–9.
18 Housman, *Lucan* (Oxford, 1926), p. xxxii.
19 See Bentley's notes on *PL*, I, 6; IV, 555; III, 597.
20 I, 7, 29 ff.
21 III, 18.
22 Quoted from Hugh Kenner, *The Counterfeiters* (Bloomington, Ind., 1968), p. 106, in *The Oxford Book of Literary Anecdotes*, ed. James Sutherland (Oxford, 1977), p. 291.
23 For the examples cited (and many others) see Justin Glenn, 'Psychoanalytic Writings on Greek and Latin Authors, 1911–60', *Classical World*, 66 (1972), pp. 129–45, and 'Psychoanalytic Writings on Classical Mythology and Religion', *Classical World*, 70 (1976), pp. 225–47; and Richard S. Caldwell, 'Selected Bibliography on Psychoanalysis and Classical Studies', *Arethusa*, 7 (1974), pp. 115–34.
24 See Robert Perceval Graves, *Life of Sir William Rowan Hamilton*, vol. 1 (Dublin, 1882), pp. 652, 348; vol. 2 (Dublin, 1885), pp. 434–5.
25 In *A Mathematician's Apology* (Cambridge, 1941), pp. 24–5.
26 Michael Polyani, in *Personal Knowledge* (London, 1958), pp. 186–7.
27 *Republic*, 602b.

CHAPTER FOUR   PHILOSOPHERS

1 Diogenes Laertius, *Pythagoras*, 8, 21.
2 D–K, i, frag. 42, cf. 57 and 106.
3 See chapter Two, n. 3. In general on Greek attitudes to truth in poetry see Harriott, pp. 112–20.
4 *Satires*, X, 174.
5 *Theogony*, 27–8.
6 *Republic*, 414b–c; cf. Euripides, *Bacchai*, 326.
7 229c–230a.
8 *Republic*, 595c ff.
9 III, 10.
10 D–K, i, 545, 15, 29.
11 J. A. Hammerton, *Stevensoniana* (London, 1903), p. 79.
12 For evidence that Wordsworth altered autobiographical material for poetic reasons see Press, p. 204.
13 II, 8, 10.
14 7, 14.
15 Aristotle, *Rhetoric*, III, 3, 4.
16 On the topic among modern English-speaking authors see

Abrams, *passim*. On the mirror as an emblem of misleading images see *Classical Review*, n.s., 4 (1954), pp. 82–5.

17 III, 2, 18 ff.
18 V, 1, 12–17.
19 D–K, ii, frags 18, 21; cf. Cicero, *De Div.*, I, 37; Horace, *Ars Poetica*, 295–6, and (on Greek poetic madness in general) Dodds, chapter 3 and Harriott, chapter 4.
20 245a.
21 1455a 32–4.
22 Chapter 15.
23 Oliver St John Gogarty, *William Butler Yeats: a Memoir* (Dublin, 1963), p. 23.
24 Frag. 137 in C. M. Bowra, *Pindari Carmina*, 2nd ed. (Oxford, 1947).
25 See index to W. A. Hammond's *Aristotle's Psychology* (London, 1902).
26 *Life of Apollonius*, VI, 19.
27 Lowes, p. 95.

CHAPTER FIVE POLITICIANS AND MORALISTS

1 Quoted and effectively refuted by Harriott, p. 107.
2 *Dichtung und Wahrheit*, 3, 12 (*Jubiläum's Ausgabe*, 24, pp. 111–112).
3 1447b 17–20.
4 Plutarch, *Solon*, 29. Scholars are divided on the authenticity of this story. For Solon's alleged censorship see Diogenes Laertius, *Solon*, 59. The reason given for the ban is because 'fiction is unprofitable' (*anophelê*).
5 V, 67; VI, 21.
6 1008–9, 1032–6, 1043–56.
7 I owe this information to Mr Terrence Kirk of the University of Texas at Austin.
8 245a. *Laws*, 681e ff.
9 *Poetics*, 1454a 17–30.
10 *Republic*, 390b.
11 For the Pythagoreans and Democritos on pleasure and pain see D–K, i, 464, 34–5; ii, 183, 13–18 and 13–14; and see index to D–K (vol. iii) at *hedoné*. For Aristotle's views in his *Poetics* see the index to Ingram Bywater's ed. (Oxford, 1909) at *hedú* and cognates.
12 1104b 8 ff.; cf. Plato, *Laws*, 653 a–c.
13 For the Stoics and Epicureans see G. M. A. Grube, *The Greek and Roman Critics* (London, 1968), pp. 136, 195.
14 Strabo, I, 1, 2 and 10; I, 2, 2–3.
15 343.
16 *Preface to Shakespeare*, quoted by Abrams, p. 19.

17 'Strongly moved': cf. 'The Emotional Power of Greek Tragedy', *Proceedings of the Classical Association*, 71 (1978), pp. 25–6, and Taplin, chapter 10.
18 1336b 3.
19 See Eustathios on *Iliad*, IX, 453, and Plutarch, *Quomodo adolescentes*, 26 f.
20 Stocker: I owe this reference to Mr D. E. Hill.
21 See Pamela Hansford Johnson, *On Iniquity: Some Personal Reflections arising out of the Moors Murders* (London, 1967). As this note is being written, newspapers report that a schoolboy in Cheshire has burned himself to death in imitation of a similar self-immolation in a film called *The Bloody Theatre*.
22 *Tennyson*, vol. 1, p. 196.

CHAPTER SIX   TWENTY-SIX FALLACIES

1 *Soph. Elench.*, 5, 167b ff.; *Poetics*, 1455a 1, 1460a 20; cf. *Rhetoric*, 1392b 16 ff. and 1401b 20 ff. and Dorothy L. Sayers, *Unpopular Opinions* (London, 1946), p. 185.
2 Leaf, *Iliad*, II, 595 n. 2.
3 *Deipnosophists*, I, 10d–e.
4 1450b 16, cf. 1449b 25–8 (see Gudeman's note).
5 I, 2, 9.
6 For these remarks by Wordsworth and Carlyle see Abrams, pp. 290, 291 and 385 n. 90.
7 Abrams, p. 291. See further in his index at 'Inspiration', Press, chapter 3, and Harding, chapters 2–3.
8 Quoted by E. R. Dodds in *Time was Away*, ed. Terence Brown and Alec Reid (Dublin, 1974), p. 36. Cf. Harding, p. 15, for other examples of automatic inspiration. But poets have also been known to make prose drafts of their poems: see *ibid.*, pp. 68–9.
9 *De Comp.*, 25.
10 See F. Budgen, *James Joyce and the Making of Ulysses*, 2nd ed. (London, 1934), p. 20.
11 *Art*, pp. 315, 317.
12 *De Gloria Ath.*, 346; cf. 18a. For other classical references see D. A. Russell, ed., 'Longinus', *On the Sublime* (Oxford, 1964) on section 17, 2; cf. Harriott, pp. 142–4.
13 *Nemeans* I, 5; cf. *Isthmians*, II, 45.
14 *Greek Metaphor*, revised reprint (New York, 1976), pp. 63–9.
15 See *The Gentle Art of Making Enemies*, 4th ed. (London, 1906), p. 45.
16 1461a 4–9.
17 Epistle to Titus, 1, 12.
18 *Hamlet*, I, 3, 78–80.
19 1471.

20 Taplin, pp. 166–7.
21 For many more false etymologies see H. W. Fowler, *A Dictionary of Modern English Usage* (Oxford, 1937), pp. 665–6.
22 See *Echoes from Kottabos*, ed. R. Y. Tyrrell and Sir Edward Sullivan (London, 1906), pp. 279–90.
23 *Richard II*, II, 1, 74.
24 Matthew 16, 18.
25 See E. R. Dodds's edition (Oxford, 1959), p. 18.
26 Information from the late Professor George O'Brien.
27 *Ars Poetica*, 60–1.
28 Wimsatt, *Leopards*, p. 39.
29 Collingwood, p. 71.
30 Collingwood, p. 69.
31 *Tennyson*, vol. 2, p. 17.
32 See *Dantis Aligherii Epistolae*, ed. Paget Toynbee, 2nd ed. (Oxford, 1966), x. 7 (p. 173).
33 See W. B. Stanford, *The Ulysses Theme*, 2nd ed. (Oxford, 1968), chapter 14.
34 Quoted in T. A. Sebeok, *Myth: a Symposium* (Bloomington, Ind., 1963), pp. 105–6.
35 A. E. Taylor, *Plato*, 2nd ed. (London, 1960), p. 18.
36 Boswell's *Life*, chapter 44 (7 April 1778).
37 Dodds, *passim*.
38 *The Bacchae of Euripides* (London, 1904), pp. 53, 91.
39 See *New Statesman*, 18 June 1967.
40 S. H. Bell, *Within our Province* (Belfast, 1972), p. 67.
41 See *The Coinage of Saorstát Éireann* (Dublin, 1928), pp. 1–7.
42 Aelian, *Varia Historia*, 14, 8.
43 See V. Lawford in *The Cornhill*, winter 1956–7, p. 95.
44 *Poetics*, 1460a 17–18.
45 Christopher Hassall in *Rupert Brooke* (London, 1972), p. 341.
46 'Swinburne', p. 399.
47 See Lowes, p. 442 n. 64.
48 L. V. Ryan, *Roger Ascham* (Stanford, Calif., 1963), p. 197.
49 Paul Valéry, *Autres Rhumbs* (Paris, 1934), p. 143.
50 Graves, p. 15, quoted by Press, p. 234.
51 Quoted to me by Professor William Calder III from oral tradition, comparing the strictures on doctrinaire analogists in Wilamowitz, *Geschichte der Philologie* (Leipzig, 1921), pp. 40–1.
52 Frag. 191 in J. M. E. Edmonds, *The Fragments of Attic Comedy*, vol. 2 (Leiden, 1959).
53 1451b 23–4.
54 This view is strongly argued by Taplin, p. 162.
55 *Politics*, 1342a 18 ff.; cf. *Poetics*, 1461b 28.
56 See the edition by M. Sadleir and F. Page (Oxford, 1950), pp. 92–3.
57 Spender, pp. 57–8.

58 Cited by C. Day Lewis, *The Poetic Image* (London, 1947), p. 71.
59 Dedicatory Epistle to *The Rival Ladies*. I owe this and the previous quotation to the study of poetic form in Press, chapter 4.
60 Spender, p. 53.
61 Horace, *Satires*, I, 5, 87; Martial, *Epigrams*, IX, 2, 13; cf. Athenaeus, *Deipnosophists*, 7, 284e.
62 *Essay on Criticism*, 350–3.
63 See especially Wimsatt, *Icon*, pp. 3–20. He has qualified his strictures on intentionalism in *Leopards*, pp. 11–39. *The Princeton Encyclopedia of Poetry and Poetics* (Princeton, 1975) has good bibliographies for the intentional and affective fallacies.
64 Wimsatt, *Icon*, p. 29.
65 Athenaeus, *Deipnosophists*, I, 22a.
66 339b ff.; cf. 341e and 347e. See further in Harriott, pp. 144–6.
67 See especially *The Princeton Encyclopedia* and Wimsatt, *Icon*, pp. 21–39.
68 A. J. A. Waldock, *Sophocles the Dramatist* (Cambridge, 1951), pp. 15–16.
69 H. D. F. Kitto in *Poiesis* (Berkeley, 1966), pp. 14–16, 21, 202.
70 Plutarch, *De Gloria Ath.*, 347e.
71 Cited by Seumas O'Sullivan, *Essays and Recollections* (Dublin, 1944), p. 66.
72 L. C. Knight in *Explorations* (London, 1963).
73 *The Waverley Pageant* (London, 1932), pp. 38–40.
74 Muriel Spark in a BBC interview on 25 September 1970.
75 Graham Greene in *The Observer*, 12 March 1970. For further examples of authors being possessed by the characters they are creating, see Harding, pp. 17–18, 46–7.
76 *Essay on the Dramatique Poetry of the last Age*, appendix to *The Conquest of Granada* (1672).
77 Quoted by J. Shawcross, *Shelley's Literary and Philosophical Criticism* (Oxford, 1909), p. 153.
78 See *Sound of Greek*, pp. 34, 46 n. 38 and 108–12.
79 See ibid., pp. 34, 108–10.
80 100. Cf. Dodds on *Bacchai*, 888.
81 I have taken this and the two following quotations from English literature from Press, pp. 144, 148, and I am indebted to him for several other points in this section. For authors as visualizers see Harding, pp. 29–32.
82 *Agamemnon*, 494–5.
83 *Macbeth*, I, 7, 35–8.
84 Press, p. 145 makes this distinction.
85 See Gudeman's note on *Poetics*, 1460a 15.
86 *Spectator*, no. 411 (1712) quoted by Press, p. 144, who in turn cites Michael Roberts, *Critique of Poetry* (London, 1934), pp. 45–59. See further in Press, chapter 5.

87 *The Music of Poetry* (Glasgow, 1942), p. 28, cited by Press, p. 118.
88 See Harding, pp. 64–8.
89 See *Sound of Greek*, pp. 1–3 (with the correction that Alexander the Great, not Julius Caesar, is the first silent reader to be unambiguously recorded in Greek history: see Plutarch, *On the Fortune of Alexander*, 340a; I owe this correction to Miss Mary Renault). Robert Frost has much to say against the silent reading of poetry: see the index to his *Letters* at 'Sentence sounds' and 'Sound of sense'.
90 Margot Asquith, *Autobiography*, vol. 1 (London, 1920), p. 198.
91 *De Sublimitate*, 39.
92 'Swinburne', p. 387.
93 *Art*, pp. 162–3.
94 Lewis, *Surprised by Joy* (London, 1957), p. 109. Other testimonies to what Wordsworth called the lost 'living voice' of classical literature (*Prelude*, vi, 94 ff.) are given in my *Sound of Greek*, pp. 134–5. See also Frost, *Letters*, p. 107.
95 Taplin, p. 165. But I cannot fully agree with his 'ritual fallacy' (pp. 161–2) – 'that Greek tragedy is in one way or another a *ritual* event'. Despite his arguments it seems to me that the setting of tragedy in the precinct of Dionysos at his greatest festival in the presence of all the greater priests and with an altar in the centre of the orchestra was bound to give it some ritualistic atmosphere, though the content of the plays was independent of it.

CHAPTER SEVEN THE FREEDOM OF POETRY

1 J. F. Auerbach, *Mimesis* (Princeton, 1953), p. 13.
2 Taken from *Gods and Fighting Men* by Lady Gregory (London, 1904), pp. 442–4.
3 In the October section of his *Shepheards Calendar*.
4 *Ars Poetica*, 102–3.
5 *Poetics*, 1455a 30–2.
6 *Letters*, p. 199.
7 Graves, p. 1.
8 Letter to Thomas Butts, 25 April 1803. Cf. Abrams, p. 215 and Harding, p. 15.
9 See Abrams, p. 214, and pp. 189–93 for modern theories of inspiration.
10 Spender, p. 60.
11 Sir Robert Ball. Professor Patrick Wayman kindly confirmed the astronomical fact for me.
12 'The Decay of Lying', *Intentions*, 12th ed. (London, 1918), p. 29.

Index

Index